Index

Preface
Prologue

Chapter

Preface:

Over the years as I lived through my various life experiences I have often thought of writing about my many different careers and the things I learned from each one and the life experiences they each gave me. My education came from mostly the "School of Hard Knocks." Each step in my learning process helped me to the next step and to the success I was able to achieve, not only in my business life but in learning to live life to the fullest. Along the path I was able to help many others succeed and that has given me fulfillment and joy.

My various careers gave me the opportunity to travel and I have been fortunate to have visited over 30 countries and most of them for free.

My motivation to finally write my life story was sparked and encouraged by my son Aron and my future step daughter Ma Li on a visit to Beijing China in the spring of 2007. It all happened over dinner one night in a private dining room with my two beautiful women soon to become my new family. Our conversation centered on education and career choices as Ma Li was just entering college and had not yet decided what career path to choose. I asked her if her intention in the future was to live and work in China or did she think she would want to work and live in any country of her choice.

We discussed her career choices if she remained in China and as well career choices that are transportable. We talked about various careers and I explained to her that she must choose a career that she would love to do. I also told her that if she chose a career and later found that this is not what she would enjoy doing for the rest of her life that she should change. I explained that I had met many people who hated their jobs but stuck with it for 40 years and never experienced the fulfillment in their lives that they should have had and how different their lives could have been.

I explained that whatever field or career you choose that you should read a book a month on your chosen career and that by doing so you would become an expert in a few years.

Ma Li asked me how many different careers or jobs I had experienced and I chuckled and took a napkin and made a list, it totaled over 25. Her mother started to laugh and when I asked why she was laughing she said that she had experienced

close to 20 different jobs in her struggle to survive in her short life span of 42 years.
My future step daughter Ma Li then said to me someday I would love to hear all about your life and experiences and that is what helped me to decide to put as they used to say "pen to paper," on in the modern world open Word and start my two finger typing.

Prologue:

We all have a whole bunch of different experiences that happen in our lives but it's what we learn and do with them that will determine the type of life we will enjoy. There is only a range of experiences we go through in life, successes, failures, get things, lose things, good relationships, bad relationships, career choices, life and ultimately death…that what life's all about.

I'm going to share in this my Life Story lessons I learned both in my personal and business life and it is my hope that the reader will benefit and learn from my experiences, successes and failures on how to live an extraordinary life.

In reading my life story I hope it stimulates you to reflect upon your own life, your business and personal experiences and that you share it with others that are important to you. It is my hope that it also stimulates you to write your own life story.

Whether you are young and entrepreneurial and have not yet had a long career or whether you are older and had a more traditional career or whether you are in the process of changing careers there are lessons here for everyone.

If you think you had an extraordinary or even an average life and that's fine there are still lessons and experiences you can share.

 I am now approaching my mid eighty's and never really retired. It's not in my makeup to ever retire as I do not know what I would do if I could not continue my learning and be involved in fun projects. I would get very bored quickly.

 It's not that that I don't have other interests to keep me busy. We live on a beautiful hobby farm with my two horses, dog and cat so my life is full.

To be able to always do something to keep my mind active is most important to me. You probably heard the saying "a body in motion tends to stay in motion" for me a "mind in motion also tends to stay in motion". To continually learn and do new and challenging projects is what my life has been all about. I hope some of the lessons I learned will help you in your personal and business life.

One of the things I truly believe and learned in my lifetime is that everyone is a sales person in one way or another and that we were all born with some sales skills, it's what we do to improve them is what makes us more successful. It might sound like a cliché but there is not anything you do that you are not dealing with people and selling them ideas, physical products and or services both in your business and personal life.

This book is for everyone, what you take out of it will be different than what someone else will. There are life and business lessons here for everyone and I would encourage you to approach this book with the same kind of open mind that I approached things in my entire life. Believe me if I would have thought at the start of my career that things would always be the same as they were that's 60 years ago I'd be in pretty bad shape. I probably would have chosen a traditional career doing the same things for 40 years. There are many people like that that strive for an ordinary life and there is nothing wrong with that and there are others who strive for adventure and challenges.

I never wanted an ordinary life and if you want to live an extraordinary life than this book will have meaning for you.

In today's world there is no longer job security and you must continue learning new skills as you probably will change careers several times. I believe that everyone should learn how to leverage themselves and the best way I know is to have a home based business in addition to your every day career.

I'm not done yet as I am in the process of writing another book as a follow up to this book that will teach additional sales skills for those who want to improve their knowledge or learn how to become a sales professional.

I have been told that this book should be read by all college and University students as it will help prepare them for the real world " The School Of Hard Knocks:

Chapter 1

Over the years when I thought of writing a book about "my life story," the question I asked myself was where I should start. I decided the best place to start is as far back as I can remember.

I can remember back when I was 2 years old; I can even remember where we lived and today more than 80 years later can describe the house down to the last detail, I can even remember where it was. I can even remember my name - a real achievement at my age. And I also remember enough to share some stories with you.

So let me give you a little history of my background and where I was born and a little background about my parents and grandparents. I was born on August 24th 1934, and my Chinese sign is the dog. I will tell you more about my Chinese connection later. I was named Norton but in my earlier years was called Norty. My parents were first generation Canadians of Jewish descent whose parents both came from Europe in the early 1900's. My mother was a typical Jewish mother whose life was centered around her 3 children; my father was a businessman working in the wholesale fruit and vegetable market, first in the family business with his father and brothers and then on his own. I was the middle child between two sisters and growing up put me in the middle of all fights and was blamed for 90%; the other 10% just seemed to disappear. My father and mother rarely practiced our religion and attended synagogue on special occasions and sometimes not even then.

My grandfather and grandmother on my father's side came from Poland; their first names were Abraham and Minnie, last name Solomon. My memories of them were that they were cold and unemotional and unable to show or express love and warmth even to their new grandchildren. The most time I ever spent with them was when they called each spring to climb their lilac tree in their back yard to cut flowers for them, and the other times is when my grandfather felt an ache or pain he would call my mother to send me over to rub him down with Menard's liniment. He had all his own hair, teeth and a body of a 40 year old until he died in his late 80's. My grandmother passed away first in her late seventies. After that, he lived alone for awhile and then with some other woman. I believe that I acquired his genes but not his taste in women.

My grandparents on my mother's side came from Romania, and, believe it or not, their first names were Abraham and Minnie, and their last name was also Solomon. Both grandparents had a daughter named Fay, and each had a son named Issie. They were the total opposite of my father's parents they were loving and warm and showed their love to their children and grandchildren, and from them, I have many loving memories.

So, how my father and mother met each other was another interesting story in itself. Both families booked a reservation at the same hotel in Ste.Agathe in the Laurentians one summer, and while on vacation my grandmother on my mother's side received a letter from whom she thought was her son Issie but could not understand what he was writing about and a few days later met the other Solomon's and found out they also had a son named Issie, and that is how both families met.

But back to my memories of where we lived. We lived in a flat on Jeanne Mance between St.Viateur and Bernard with a winding outside staircase to a balcony on the second floor which had 3 doors, one on the left and right and a third in the middle for the upper flats. We lived on the right. When you entered, there was a living room on the right side and attached by way of an archway was the master bedroom; down a long hall was the kitchen and off to the right a small bedroom which was for us kids, my 2 sisters and me. Off the kitchen was a balcony the length of the kitchen overlooking a back courtyard and at the end of the kitchen was a door to a wooden shed with a staircase to the back lane. Not too many years before this is where people kept their horses and wagons. Our bedroom consisted of a crib for my baby sister Bernice and a set of bunk beds for me and my older sister Eileen. The top bunk was for the one who did not pee during the night even though sometimes mistakes were made and a warm shower was a gift to the lower occupant. I can to this day take the reader to this my home of my first memories. What other memories flood my mind about my early years living on Jeanne Mance. Many were good but some remained a mark on my life that caused me much grief and hardships that I had to deal with in my adult life.

The worst thing my young mind remembered was the weekly arguments between my father and mother or should I say between my mother and father and the effect it had on my life in later years that resulted in the failure of my first marriage and many other relationships.

My father was a hard worker who for most of his life worked in the wholesale fruit and vegetable market, most of the time in business for himself. But he had a weakness or an addiction to gambling. So here's what happened as I remember; after working hard and long hours each week, he would get together with his cronies Friday nights and play poker or go to the race track and some weeks gamble away his week's earnings. Next scene was he would come home in the wee hours and the arguments would follow after my mother waited all night for him to show and then to find out if he won or lost his week's earnings. The yelling would center around if there was enough money left to feed us children for the week.

  Arguments nearly always ended with my father leaving and sometimes not coming home for days. What effect did all this have on my young mind? As the years went by, I dreamt and worried that my father would not be there for me or my sisters, and this led me to build a wall of protection around myself to insure that I would not be hurt by anything or anyone ever. As I lost trust in him, I found that could not even call him father or dad as I did not believe he would be there for me. As I look back, what a burden for a young boy to carry and what a loss to both of us for I carried this feeling for most of my adult life.

My early memories were not all bad; there were many good memories. Jeanne Mance was a mixture of many cultures in those years, and the street was alive with many different sounds and smells. Bread was delivered by Wonder Bread with a team of ponies, and the bread man would come to the door with his basket of fresh bread, rolls and cakes, enough to make your mouth water. The ponies were in my view the most beautiful animals, well behaved and trained. Milk was delivered in glass bottles with cardboard corks the same way but with a huge horse and wagon, and in the winter as the milk sat on you balcony in the early morning it would freeze and the corks would raise up an inch or more.

My love of horses probably came from these early experiences and remain to this day as I still have 2 horses that share and fulfill my life and have given me many enjoyable experiences.

 In the summer, the city would send men to block the street in the late morning and open the fire hydrant for us kids to play and cool down.

My next memory was of hospital smells as I had managed to jump off the kitchen table when I was 4 years old and ended up with a double hernia. So off to the hospital we went and the next thing I remember was coming home and my uncle

Ben, who was my Aunt Fay's husband, bought me a little red wagon as a welcome home gift. Uncle Ben was a big strong man who to me looked and acted like a cowboy, tough on the outside but with a heart of gold. As I was his first boy nephew, we bonded, and he took me with him for weekends to Ste.Agathe where he was building a beautiful summer home on a hill overlooking Lac des Sables. He was a building contractor and built many apartments on Ste. Catherine Road near Victoria Ave. These memories take me up to the age of five when we then moved to another phase of my early life, living on St. Urbain Street near Mount Royal in the heart of the Jewish ghetto.

My first lesson in life was to protect myself from disappointment and hurt.

Lessons learned:

We all have different experiences that happen in our early lives   good and bad that could affect us in our adult lives.
My father being a gambler I decided that this was not the path I would follow.

Chapter 2

We lived on St.Urbain for a few years in a main floor duplex near Mount Royal and I attended public school right across the road. For some reason this period did not leave to much an impression on my life. The things that I can remember are that we got our first dog, a beautiful German shepherd puppy that I adored and spent most of my free time with. One afternoon when I came home from school the hall was covered in chewed-up bits and pieces of a set of encyclopedias my mother had collected over a period of years. I cleaned up the mess and took all the paper down to the basement to burn in the coal furnace and in my rush to get rid of the evidence overloaded the furnace and some paper fell out and started burning the books I had on the floor. I managed to put out the fire and get rid of all the smoke before my mother came home probably saving my dog's life. It was months before my mother discovered that the books were missing. Another time I could not find him anywhere in the house and worried that somehow he managed to slip out the door when someone came in. We looked everywhere and finally found him snuggled under a pile of clothes near the washing machine.

It was wartime and as children we knew little about the war and what could affect us if anything. Until one afternoon I heard noises coming from the sky and went outside to see the cause. I looked up and saw and heard the roar of what to me seemed to be 100's of planes filling the sky and I thought it must be the Germans and I ran back in the house and hid under the living room sofa shaking in fear. I later found out it was our planes on to England to join the war.

As a boy growing up my toys were typical boy toys, guns and a bow and arrow. One day when I was playing with a neighbor son I pointed my bow at him and let one fly and almost took out his eye. My punishment was severe and I could not sit without pain for several days. I also had to own up and apologize and give up my new toy thereby giving up my chance to become an archer and go to the Olympics, so much for my archery skills.

My grandmother and grandfather on my mother's side lived on Clark St. one block away so I spent many an afternoon with them as my mother worked and that's where I was to go after school.

The famous and infamous communist spies' husband and wife - the Rosenbergs - and their children lived across the street, When they were arrested it shook up the whole neighborhood.

My grandfather became sick and was rushed to the hospital and I was too young to visit with him. While he was in the hospital I found out that he would like a foot stool when he came home, so off to the basement I went and built him one that was to be his home coming gift. On the day he was to be released he passed away and I can remember my tears and sorrow in the loss of such a gentle loving man.

Clark Street was home to many Jewish families but on the east side of St. Lawrence Boulevard lived many French families so we had a few small fights now and then. I would go upstairs to my grandmother in tears not understanding why the French kids hated us. I remember her telling me that I should be proud of being a Jew and always stand up for myself.

Any problem I told her about she would say my grandson "the wheel turns and it will always come back to the same spoke and you never have to push it!" It did not mean much to me then but in later years it proved over and over again to be a wise truth.

After a few years Jews started to leave the Ghetto and we moved to Hutchinson Street near Fairmount, The side of the street we lived on was part of Outremont, we were getting up in the world. I attended school on Durocher Street a block from our home. The school had a mixed population of several different cultures and each had their own cliques and gangs competing with each other. I had no problems with most of them except for a few Jewish tough guys who like to pick on the smaller kids of which I was one. So being chased home and fights became a weekly thing. I could sure run like hell in those days in fact I won a medal for first place at a meet in Outremont Park where out of 3 races I only ran the last two and beat everyone out. I ran so fast that I could not stop at the end of track and jumped over a park bench into a policeman's arms.

The school's main floor had a large area that was divided by a row of posts that became the line of no crossing as the boys had to stay on one side and the girls on the other during recess. One day as I was trying my running shoe laces and looking over at the girls I did not see another boy being chased and as I stood up he smashed right into my face causing my left eye to swell up. It looked like the shape of an egg and took a long time to heal and even today one eyelid is higher than the other.

Guess what it became, a place for the tough guys to take aim making it grow even larger. I finally decided it was time to get tough and listen to my grandmother's advice and stand up for myself. A few days later I met one of the tough guys whose name was Howie Bell at our local candy store on the corner of Fairmount and Hutchison and told him that if he wanted to fight me without his gang now was the time.

The owner of that candy store was a grouchy old fart and he would try and cheat us when we brought bottles back for refunds. So we decided to teach him a lesson. Bottles were stored in the back of the store in a shed which was left open some days so we would take some bottles from the shed back to the front of the store for refunds and buy candy with the profits. When he was really mean we would put a stink bomb under the counter. For better or worse, boys will almost always be boys.

Back to the fight out we went and before we started I warned him not to hit me in the eye, I guess that was the wrong thing to say because as you guessed his first punch was a direct hit. I went wild and picked him up and put him over a spiked fence and if a man had not seen this and rushed over to his aid I could have broken his back. The result of this fight quickly spread and news found its way to the other tough guys and I was no longer picked on. I had learned to stand on my own. As I was now considered a tough guy we became friends.

I was now 11 years old and started to work after school and on weekends at a grocery store owned by Mr. Shapiro on St.Viateur near Park Ave right next to where the bagel store is today. My job was filling the shelves with goods that were not rationed as rationed goods were stored in the back for the good customers. It was war time. Some rationed things were sugar, ketchup, butter, halvah, etc. I also delivered groceries in a 3 wheel bike with a large metal basket in front. Being short I had to stand up to peddle and being small I had trouble lifting the boxes of grocery out of the basket and sometimes had to empty the box to lift it out.

Between my meager salary and tips I managed to save enough to buy my first bicycle by the time I was 12 and it was a beauty, a CCM with a basket in front and a chrome carrier in the back complete with a bell and lights I was mobile.

One day our landlord's son told me about his cousin who owned Park Bakery on Park Ave, who because of a shortage of shortening would have to close down as he could not bake cakes or pies. I said I knew where to buy a lot of shortening and off

I went on my bike to all the small grocery stores in the area and bought up all that I could carry in my bike's basket. I sold the lot to Park bakery for a small profit and went back for more. I was immediately hired for more pay then I was earning at the grocery store and my first job was to clean the delivery truck from all the bread crumbs that fell through the wooden racks. I was then promoted to stuff the jelly donuts, my favorite job as I ate probably as much as I stuffed and to this day they are still my choice of donut. From stuffing donuts to up front selling breads and cakes my first real sales job.

When I was 11 years old my father and mother purchased some land in Ste. Agathe from my uncle Ben and started to build a summer cottage. Around the same time my father and my uncle Ben were driving on Decarie Blvd one night just north of Cremazie and noticed a crowd at a car dealership, and out of curiosity stopped to see what was happening. It was an auction selling a 1929 Packard touring car similar to what Hitler was chauffeured about in. Guess what he got caught up in the bidding and bid once too often and we ended up the owners. With gas rationing at the time he won the bidding for $500 dollars. The car was built like a tank with 720 truck size tires and a double windshield, so when you got in the back seat you had your own windshield, it was also a convertible.

When I was 12 my father taught me how to drive the Packard around Lac des sables and I became a quick learner because every time I would jerk the clutch because I did not use the pedal properly I would get a whack in the back of my head.

When I wanted to go down the hill to the beach I would ask for the keys and my father would toss them to me and while my mother argued that I should not drive the car by myself away I went. As time went by instead of just going up and down the hill I would drive around the lake but turn around before reaching the village for the fear of being caught by the police. My turn around spot was at Clark's stables. I would stop and see the horses and my love for these animals grew.

 My father's best friend was Al Conroy who had a horse that he kept at a stable near Beaver Lake on Mount Royal and one day we went to see his horse. When we pulled into the parking lot Al came out of the stable to greet us, I asked where his horse was and he whistled and the horse came running out of the stable, right to his side. He was magnificent color, liver brown and his coat shone bright in the sunlight. He put me in the saddle and I thought that I had died and went to heaven. He walked the horse around the yard and I saw the world from a different perspective. I knew someday I would own one of these beautiful animals. Later that year the horse developed heaves which was caused by bad hay and he offered it to me to take up to Ste.Agathe where he could eat fresh grass. Before we could arrange transportation and build a barn he got worse and Al decided to put him down. I was heartbroken as I pictured myself riding through the meadows and owning my first horse. Al Conroy was also heartbroken and never rode again. Time went by quickly as I was always busy at school and learning for my Bar Mitzvah or working. I first attended Talmud Torah and one week was appointed locker monitor and as I was checking to make sure they were locked, one came off the wall and smashed into the back of my head. I was rushed to the hospital and had to stay home for over a month healing. When I was well enough to go back to school the first thing I did was check if the locker had been attached to the wall and guess what happened it fell again and I refused to go back for my Bar Mitzvah learning so my parents hired a private tutor who came to our home 3 times a week. To this day I don't know if it knocked any sense into to me.

 When I was 13 years old my father had a friend that had a fruit and vegetable store on Ontario St. east and needed help on the weekends. What an experience this was. To this day I have never seen any store as busy as this one was, We had to refill the fruit and vegetable racks continually, the owner ran back and forth to the wholesaler all day to bring more fresh produce. I had to empty the cash register and put the money in brown paper bags every hour. I caught one of the employees pocketing money and reported it to the owner and he was fired.

When I was 14 my father bought a grocery store on Park Ave. near Milton that had a meat counter, fruit and vegetable area and grocery section complete with license to sell beer. My father looked after the fruit department, I because of my previous experience working for Mr. Shapiro was to look after the grocery dept. and stock the shelves after school and weekends and my mother was the cashier. We rented out the meat counter to a butcher and we were a full service food store. Sundays I would take stock and make up an order for all grocery items and on Monday's at recess I would call in the order to the wholesaler to be picked up Tuesday afternoon after school. The area around Milton housed a lot of students who attended McGill University with many fraternity houses and a fair number of hookers who both ordered many cases of beer and groceries. It was an interesting area for a young boy to experience.

I worked long hard hours and this experience taught me that life was not easy and to succeed at whatever you chose to do you needed to put in the hours and effort. Life in Montreal in the late 1940's and 50's was much different than it is today. Everyone from all the different cultures got along with each other; we were all Canadians and did not ask the Government to change laws and rules to suit our different cultures. There was no talk of separation, life was good.

Lessons learned:

"What I learned was not to be afraid of hard work and what it takes to become successful"

Over the years I have met many people who hated their jobs but only a few who were afraid of hard work.

Chapter 3

Life isn't about finding yourself. Life is about creating yourself. George Bernard Shaw

I was now in High school and attended Baron Byng High School on St. Urbain, and this led to a whole new experience in my life.

The school's population consisted of many Jewish street kids like me not from wealthy families and as part of this social group I had to learn to make my own way. We also had a mix of many different cultures and races. Racism did not exist at the time in our school.

When I turned 14 and was in 8th grade and working every afternoon, it became more difficult for me to be at school, at work and take a bus or streetcar to and from school and home, so my father decided maybe it was time for me to obtain a driver's license, so down to the license bureau we went and applied or should I say lied…I became 17 years old very quickly as in those days there were no computers, and my father's verification was all that was needed. Since I had learned to drive when I was 12 in my father's Packard touring car, I now was able to drive the store's delivery pickup truck or family car when needed.

In May when my father drove to Ste Agathe to open our summer cottage you had to drive up the old highway 17 and thru the village of Ste. Jerome. In passing a gas station, he saw a car for sale. When he returned to Montreal he made the mistake of telling me about it, and that same day we drove back to see it. It was a 1939 Desoto convertible with a rumble seat, yellow in color and with a white roof. It had an overdrive and a free-wheeling feature, floor stick shift, and we bought it that night for the whopping sum of $ 600 dollars. In those days, it was more than pocket change.

The convertible roof had shrunk, and the first time I opened it, it would not close. As luck would have it, it rained, and we got a free shower. Until I could afford a new roof, I carried an umbrella to be used inside the car; it was something to see. I always parked the car behind the school on Clark St. and at lunch time would drive it around the front, and my friends and some girls would take a drive or go to

Wilensky's for a salami sandwich or Schwartz's for a smoked meat sandwich for lunch. Thank God, Macdonald's did not exist then.

One day, I noticed that the car was covered in ink, and looking up, I noticed some ink on a window cell from a classroom on the top floor of the school right above my car, so a few friends and I went up and tried to get whoever was responsible to own up without luck. I found out who the culprit was over 30 years later, and that is another story.

Baron Byng opened a whole new set of experiences for me; I became class president and my main responsibility was to keep order in the class. I was later encouraged to run for student council. Never having to prepare a campaign or give a speech in front of a group scared the wits out of me, but remembering my grandmother's words "stand up for yourself". I decided to give it a try. I came close but was beat out by Maynard Shapiro who became president and later in life Dr. Maynard Shapiro but it wasn't a total loss because I became social chairman, a role I was to discover I was more suited for.

 I also joined the Senior Boy's choir as my voice had become a deep baritone. I, to this day, remember and still sing one of the songs we sang "Oh! Shenandoah"
Our choir was such a success that we performed in front of a large audience several evenings in the school auditorium which was filled to capacity. We also performed at different schools and were recorded for broadcast on local radio. On the night of our last big performance and after our last bows, the crowds and students all walked up Park Ave singing and just having some fun, some walking down the middle of the street and blocking traffic. Some irate motorist must have called the cops as dozens of police cars suddenly appeared trying to control the crowds.
 I and a few friends decided to grab a smoked meat sandwich with a few of the girls at the deli on the corner of Mount Royal and Park Ave next to the YMHA. When we walked out of the deli, we were surrounded by 3 police cars, arrested and taken to the police station. We had done nothing wrong but probably were an easy catch, so off to the caboose we went. We were kept there until 2.30 am and then driven home by a police officer. What a shock when my parents answered the door. We were concerned that we would have a police record, but our alderman intervened, and all charges were dropped.

In June, I was driving to school to write my exams and stopped at a stop sign on Clark St., and while stopped, a delivery truck owned by Star Trucking smashed into the back of my car damaging my bumper and rumble seat; lucky for me it was witnessed by a man who was just going to have lunch and who happened to own a body shop repair garage right at that corner. I was in tears, but he said not to worry that he would look after contacting the insurance company, fix it and repaint the whole car, and it would look like new. A few days later, he asked me what color paint I would like, and I chose a metallic green. When I went to pick up the car, it looked as if it had just come out of the showroom. The only thing that was still needed was a new roof which the garage owner said he would do, and I could pay him a little each week. To this day, I still dream about my first car and have even tried to find one to restore.

In grade 9, I decided what the school needed was a big school dance, so I put together a business plan or should I say a Norton plan to hold the biggest and best dance the school ever had. I then approached Mr. Henderson, our assistant school Principal, and explained what I wanted to do. His comments were that it was too big a project and that the school simply did not have the funds to support it. I persisted, and he told me to prepare a written plan and come back to him at a later date. I guess that was his way of saying, get lost Norton. But lost I did not get; instead, I prepared a written plan and budget, and he then took me to see the Principal for approval. My plan called for me to pre sell enough tickets to cover all costs before I would get final approval. Undaunted, I convinced every class to pre purchase 30 tickets, and we were off to the races.

My plan was to hire a live band, something that was never done in the school's history as well as an M.C. and some entertainment. I hired Lenny Rubin and his band and then called CJAD and hired their most popular radio disc jockey Don Cameron. When I called the radio station to make an appointment and negotiate fees, I was asked to meet him at the radio station. I arrived a few minutes before he got off the air and told the receptionist who I was; she told me to wait in the reception area. A few minutes later, he appeared and asked the receptionist where Mr. Solomon was as he expected to meet with an older man. She pointed at me, 5'5' weighing 120 lbs and 14 years old but with a baritone voice of a 30 year old. We talked, and at one point Don suggested that I should consider becoming a radio announcer. We came to terms, and he became my M.C. for the big dance.

As the big night approached, every class got involved decorating the gym with balloons and crepe paper. The two snack bars were stocked, and we were ready. When the doors opened, the crowds of students and their dates rushed in like a tidal wave; these were the pre sold ticketed ones. Next came a second influx of others who purchased tickets at the door, and we had to stop selling as we were filled to capacity. We had to obey fire laws and only allow a given number in. The dance was so successful that not only did we break even but made a tidy profit. Baron Byng high school was a mixture of different cultures, and as such in those days,

 there were always some disputes which normally took place at lunch time. I as social director came up with an idea: why not keep the students busy at lunch time. I set up music for dancing in the courtyard, and there were no more fights.

One of the students showed up driving his father's car with or without permission and decided at lunchtime to take a joyride with another student and while driving up Park Avenue between Mount Royal and Pine Avenue he hit a street car head on. The driver survived with no injuries but the other student died from his injuries. We all were devastated and I decided that we needed to set up a scholarship fund in his memory. I collected $1500 and we presented this scholarship fund to his parents at his funeral.

Every student had their favorite teacher, and mine was Mr. Stewart who taught us first in grade 8. He would take us out for Chinese food and even invite some students to his home. He lived with his mother and was not married to my knowledge. As I was class President that year, we all decided that if Mr. Stewart was not to be promoted to grade 9 we wouldn't either, and it was my job to convince the powers to be to promote him .Yea! He not only became our grade 9 teacher but also our grade 10 as well.

In grade 9 one of the classes we had to attend was mechanical drawing. Our teacher was a strict tough ex army major who ruled with a heavy hand and heavy ruler. He would start the class asking us who wanted to learn and if not we could leave, so 90% of the class left and off to the Seville theatre we would go to see some comedy acts. I remember that only 2 students completed that class and today I still have a hard time drawing a straight line. At the theatre we would sit in the front row and suck lemons and the performers would drool watching us, boy! were those fun days.

When I turned 15, my father was forced to sell the store as the church next door that owned the property wanted to expand, and we were out of business. Around that time, things became a little financially tight for the family, and we moved to a basement apartment on Cote St. Catherine Road near Victoria Ave owned by my uncle Ben. Around the corner was a drug store of which half was a soda bar with a counter and some 20 stools. The owner was a man with a handicap with one bad leg which made it difficult for him to stand and work long hours on the cement floor. I was hired and became a short order cook and soda jerk working most days after school and weekends. That summer when he became sick I managed the soda bar by myself. I hired and fired staff and caught some stealing. Managing and running a business came naturally to me at age 15. I was a tough boss. We served hot dogs, hamburgers, sodas, milk shakes and ice cream and did a thriving business.

There was a taxi stand across the road, and all the drivers would have lunch or just pass some time at the counter joking with each other over a coke or soda. There was one driver who must have weighed 350 lbs. and when he ordered hot dogs it was a minimum of 4 and no matter how much mustard I put on the dogs he always asked for more. So one day with the o.k. from the other drivers, I decided to play a joke on him, and instead of regular mustard, I mixed up a batch of Keens hot mustard and loaded his hot dogs. All the other drivers watched as he took his first bite which was one half of the hot dog and a load of hot mustard his face lit up, we all laughed so hard some fell off the stools. I thought he was going to kill me but he took it in good humor and never asked for more mustard again.

It was while we were living here that I had my first crush on a beautiful girl a couple of years older than me. One day, my sister Eileen and I were sitting on the front steps of the apartment when a young lady walked by. I remember clearly that she wore a pair of jeans and a pink angora sweater. I thought she was the most beautiful girl that I had ever laid eyes on. But on she walked out of sight, but as luck would have it, a few minutes later, it started to rain quite hard, and she came running back. My sister invited her to join us on the apartment steps, and we all talked; her name was Sally. She had a British accent that sounded beautiful to me, and for some reason, I still love women with British accents. I think the men sound a little queer. My sister and Sally became friends and I was just just the younger brother. When the rain stopped, I offered to walk her home, and she accepted. She worked as a cashier at the Snowdon Theater. Some nights, I would walk her home, and we became friends. Then she disappeared, and I found out she had moved back to England, my first lost love. She corresponded with my sister for a few years but never with me.

My boss at the soda fountain became seriously ill, and they put the business up for sale. I was only 16 at the time and tried to convince my father to let me buy it as the owner was prepared to accept monthly payments from me. I could have probably retired at age 21 with the profits, but I wasn't allowed to quit school.

A few friends and I decided to apply for jobs at Steinberg's grocery on Queen Mary Street and I was hired first as a bag boy. On Saturday nights, some of us bag boys were given the job of removing all the vegetables and fruit from the counters and taking them down to the walk- in cooler for the weekend. I soon ended up as the supervisor of the group and was noticed by the produce manager and was promoted to work in that department. I chose my friends to help empty the shelves each Saturday, and when we finished, we organized a feast of every fruit, and this became our dinner. Some of the staff in the grocery department wanted to join us so we cut a deal; they brought cookies and cakes to the feast.

I was now 17, and Steinberg's had a second small store just west of Decarie Blvd, and I was asked to replace the produce manager when he went on vacation. I was responsible to order fresh produce every day and manage the rest of the staff. I started to think maybe this was a career I should consider as managers made a decent living. I was still working on an hourly wage and approached a supervisor to be put on a salary and in training to become a full time manager. I waited all summer for a decision and when none came, I decided that this was not the company I would want to make a career with; it was time to move on.

One of my father's friend's sons's who was 21 started selling baby feeding tables and told me about his experiences selling. I thought I could do this and asked him to arrange a meeting with his sales manager. When I met the manager, he tried to discourage me, thinking that I was too young. He said I would need a car assuming that I did not have one but when I told him I did he decided to give me a chance. The table was called Baby Butler, and I had to purchase my sample which we carried to presentations. Leads were purchased at 10 cents each and came from the hospitals from new births. The manager's policy was that the representative with the most sales each week would have first choice on the area he or she preferred to work.

I remember my first call on Ridgeway Drive, off of Cote des Neiges in an apartment building. I knocked on the door and was greeted by a petite woman who when I told her who I represented invited me in. She said her husband was just finishing his dinner and that I should set up the table and he would join us in a few

minutes. A few minutes later out he came; the man was huge weighing at least 300 lbs. I started my presentation describing the table's features, and at each feature, he stated that he did not feel a need to buy a highchair or any other table as he was from a large family that never had a high chair, and they all survived. I took out a newspaper article that told the story of a baby falling out of a high chair and spitting his skull. I then told him that our special designed table would never tip, and even if he sat on one corner, the other legs would never leave the ground. I did not think he would try and sit on one corner but when he sat down I figured that's the end of my sample, but to both our surprise, the other legs stayed on the ground.
 Here is when I became a salesman. I did not say another word; I packed up my table and told him that I would be back in the area next Tuesday and if he wished to purchase a table for his new son, he would need a $ 12.00 deposit. When I called back the following Tuesday and when I knocked on the door, he was ready with his deposit. I had made my first sale, and I learned "he who speaks last loses" or that there is a time in any presentation that you need to stop selling. My commission was $ 12.00 on each table sold plus a few bucks on feeding bowls and spoons. I was soon making several sales a week and beating out some of the full time representatives. This was my first experience in direct sales.
I was now in grade 11 and soon to graduate, but my grades were poor as I had spent most of my time at Baron Byng in other activities and working after school with not much time for studies. My graduation certificate was a High School Leaving Certificate, not good enough to enter university.
But looking back at my time at Baron Byng, what I learned there could not be taught at any University. I knew even at this early age who would be destined to become successful and who was doomed to lead an ordinary life.
I had a better sense of what I wanted to do in life and what I enjoyed most even at this early age.

Lessons learned:

**I DECIDED EARLY IN LIFE THAT I WAS NOT DESTINED TO BE A SCHOLAR BUT TO BE AN ENTREPRENEUR.
I LEARNED NEGOTIATING, COMMUNICATION, SELF MOTIVATION, CONFIDENCE AND SALES SKILLS AT THIS EARLY AGE.**

Everyone needs to decide what type of life they want to lead as we are all wired differently. You and only you can decide the kind of life you want. I knew I wanted the freedom to do what I enjoyed and loved and be in control of my own destiny.
Work on your weaknesses but spend more time in developing your strengths. Understand what you are good at and enjoy doing and you'll enjoy a fulfilling life.

Your weaknesses will not result in failure; your strengths will determine your success.

CHAPTER 4

Always turn a negative situation into a positive situation. Michael Jordon

Now it was time to leave the nest and safety of High School and meet the real world. Not having a clue of what the future held or what field of work I was to start my life in, I like most guys my age had to decide to get my feet wet. After my experience of working for Steinberg's grocery stores and being jerked around by the regional supervisor I decided this was not the company I wanted to build a career with the pace for me was too slow.

A friend's brother had just started a photographic distribution business as a one man operation and needed help so I decided why not as I was interested in photography and owned my first Pentax camera and had taken many photos over the past few years. He started his business above his brother's retail camera store on Craig St. near St.lawrence St. which was and still is called Simon's Cameras. The building had an apartment above that had 2 stories and a series of many small rooms that were probably bedrooms at one point. Right across the street on the corner of Clark St. was a flop house for vagrants or sailors coming off the ships. I could smell the disinfectant that was sprayed every morning. Craig St. was a life in itself with pawn shops lined along the north side of the street from St. Lawrence to La Gauchetiere Street. At night drunks would sleep in doorways or on the sidewalks. My first job was shipper and inventory stock keeper. At first it was simple as we had very little inventory therefore very little to ship. My boss was my friend Jackie Mendelson's brother whose name was Eddie Mendelson. Eddie was a super salesman and a good negotiator who was able in a short time to get distribution rights for new lines of photographic equipment. This was before the days of computers so inventory was something that you had to remember what you had and where it was kept. I must have had a photographic memory because I knew where everything was.

Shipping labels had to be typed on an old typewriter with my 2 fingers as typing was not offered at Baron Byng. We hired a secretary and I even remember her name Lilly she was very tall, sexy and well built and became a distraction for a young guy like me who was just entering his sexual prime.

 My weekly pay started at a whopping $ 22 dollars for over 40 hours of work each week so I had to sell my car and take the streetcar to work.

One morning a friend and I were on a street car commuting to work and two girls boarded one was a girl we went to school with the other I did not recognize until she spoke with a British accent, she was my sister's friend Sally back in Canada. She did not recognize me but when I mentioned my sister she remembered who I was. I was too shy to ask for her phone number and I later found out she once again moved back to England.

The work became more interesting as Eddie acquired the distribution right for the line of Hasselblad cameras and other top lines. We also were the first ones to import a line of cameras from Japan. Remember this was shortly after the war and nobody wanted to buy Japanese goods. The first camera was a knock off of a Rolleiflex twin lens camera which at the time sold for hundreds of dollars. The retail for the Yashica knock off was $ 69.95 and we couldn't give them away.

I decided to take one home over the weekend and shoot a few rolls of film and have them developed on Monday. When I saw the quality of the prints and showed the to Eddie's brother Hy who owed Simon's cameras he could not believe his eyes. But still no sales and here we were stuck with a crate full. Eddy was away on a sales trip and I came up with what I thought was a brilliant idea why not offer some of the managers at some of our clients, like Eatons, NDG Photo a camera to try for the weekend complete with 2 rolls of film that we would pay the processing for. Well they were as astonished as I was and the orders started flowing in. A first for us and a beginning of acceptance of the quality of Japanese goods. It was before Christmas and we had to fly in a shipment to fill the orders.

Within the year my salary increased to $ 40 dollars a week and the company kept adding new lines of equipment. One was a line of filters called Edna and we started promoting it at an exhibition at the Mount Royal hotel. The owner of Edna was present to help in demonstrating this new line of filters. The problem was that there were many different types of filters and attachments for the different cameras and photo shops were required to purchase a large amount complete with a huge display case as their initial order. The second problem was that with the

development of more types of filters, none of us had any knowledge on how to deal with the technical questions that would come as a result of increased sales. The owner of Edna was impressed with my skills in presenting his line as I also sold more displays then our sales reps. He offered to take me back to the U.S.A. for training I would have become the expert in filters and lenses in Canada.
 My boss refused as he was probably worried that I would know more than him and that would show him up. I had discovered that he was not open to make any improvements to any suggestions made by me or others unless it was his idea. In fact some of the suggestions I had made that he rejected he personally took ownership months later as his. This was to be his downfall in later years after building a large distributorship only to go bankrupt.

Lessons learned:

"Here was where I learned my first valuable lesson in life and in the business world…That was " if anyone tries to hold you back or get in your way of advancement it was time to move on". So, on I moved!

CHAPTER 5

Whatever you are be a good one.   Abraham Lincoln

On I moved to a new chapter in my life from a shipper to a 50% owner of a business. My father and a friend had opened a 7-11 type convenience store the year before in Valois part of Pointe.Claire near Dorval and were not doing well. I suggested that they add a counter and start serving sandwiches and coffee to increase sales. But they both had no experience in food preparation so along came the expert me. While in High School I consumed a lot of sandwiches mostly made by my own hand and many by Schwartz's deli on St.Lawrence, as well I worked as a short order cook for one year after school when I was 15 years old. We bought out the partner and I became the in-house expert. We named the restaurant "Mike and Norty's delicatessen.

I never had a cooking lesson in my life but from an early age dabbled in cooking and baking some special sauces and many jelly rolls using all the jam I could find in the house. I quickly learned to improve my cooking skills by trial and error. We started with a counter with 10 seats and gradually added several tables and our sandwich menu changed over time to serving Montreal style smoked meat and daily lunch specials as my cooking skills improved, we had a large group of steady customers who returned for breakfast and lunches every day so I must have been doing something right.

The restaurant business was not an easy one as we opened at 6am.and closed around 10pm making for a long day standing on a cement floor, 7 days a week, 365 days a year and on leap year 366 days. But it had its rewards. We never starved and made an above average income and were able to write off a lot of business and personal expenses.

Working that many hours a day was just too difficult so I figured out a schedule where we worked no more than an average of 8-9 hours. My schedule was 6am until 1.30 after the lunch hour slowed down and from 6-7.30 in the evening. This gave me a lot of free time to pursue my hobbies, boating and horseback riding.

I had a boat on lake St.Louis, a small outboard cruiser that I bought with a friend of mine his name is Bernie and mine being Norton, we named our boat the Norbern. Many an afternoon was spent on the lake.

We bought a house and now living and having our business in Valois a small town which was at the time close to many farms and open land and I again thought about horses.

The purchase of my first horse was an interesting story. One day one of my regular customers an oil delivery truck driver asked me what I was up to and I told him I went horseback riding the day before and he said why not buy your own horse? I said where would I keep it and how do you look after such an animal. I did not have room in the restaurant or in our garage at home. Just then 2 brothers who were also regulars were having a coffee, spoke up and said we have a farm on the outskirts of Dorval airport with a stable and there is another young guy that keeps his horse there. They said they would not charge me anything for keep but I could give their hired help $10.00 dollars a month to muck out and feed. While we were talking the driver went to use the pay phone and when he returned he said we were going to meet his father that night,who happened to be a cattle dealer and knew where there were several horses. I bought my first horse that very night for $ 90.00 dollars.

Peter Stevenson was the other young guy who stabled his horse at the same farm loaned me his saddle and taught me how to ride and look after my horse. We became good friends and later partners buying, training and selling horses. We owned 13 at one point. Peter was a good rider and knew how to work with them. We bought sleighs, sulkies, wagons and we had great times organizing hay rides summer and winter for our friends and some of our borders.

We had rented a farm from MOT that had a large barn and 80 acres of land, for $250 dollars a year. It had the airport radio towers on the front of the property. The only condition was we had to cut the hay to protect them from fire. Boy was this a deal. We rented some stalls and sold some of the excess hay to a trainer at Blue Bonnets race track.

When it was haying time we hired a local farmer to cut, rake and bale the hay. Eighty acres produces a lot of baled hay so we organized a hay party to bring in the hay. We had wagons, pickup trucks following the baler and believe it or not we brought in all the hay in one evening. It was something to see, two of the girls rode their horses with saddlebags full of beer so it was lift a bale have a drink. The farmer never saw hay picked-up that fast and talked about it for years.

One of our boarders worked for a film distribution company so in the summer and fall we would have movie nights every second Saturday. The barn was white washed so it became our movie screen. We set up barbeques and everyone brought their own hamburgers and hot dogs. The local police would come and join us, have a free hot dog and watch some of the latest movies.

One weekend we decided to go to a country fair in Huntington,Qc. and here is where I met a friend of one of our boarders Anne. Her name was Irene Olszewski and she had just moved from Saskatchewan. A pretty farm girl from the prairies She loved horses and we started dating.

 An old horse dealer on Cote de Liesse right next to Rolls Royce plant took a liking to Peter and suggested that he had the makings of a Ferrier. He on his own inquired about a Ferrier College in the USA for training and had me try and convince Peter that he should pursue this career.

After Peter married I kept pushing him to go but the only thing that held him back was financing, so I offered to co-sign a loan and off to California he and his new bride Susan went. He became the best Ferrier in Quebec.

One day we placed an ad in the local paper to sell one of our horses and a lady called and arranged to visit and test ride as she had just opened a riding stable in Baie D'Urfe not far from us. She showed up that afternoon and she had an English accent and when she and I were in the stall I looking at the mare I noticed a slight scar on her right cheek and here was my first love Sally once again. She was unhappily married to an accountant and horses were also her first love and she had been teaching riding in England. We became friends and when her marriage broke up had an affair for over a year before she once again returned to England.

My friends who never had the opportunity to experience the beauty of these magnificent animals first thought I was nuts but they soon not only learned to love these animals and some of them actually bought their own. The first to get hooked was Joe Winagar.

 So in between working, boating and spending time with my horses which soon became several horses my life was full. The memories I have from that period was something I will never forget ……

Riding my mare bareback with her colt running alongside through the open fields with the wind blowing in my face was one of life's wonderful experiences.

I had purchased a buckskin mare in foal and that spring and one of the most rewarding experiences was when she foaled one morning. I had spent the night in the barn awaiting the miracle. My father had to open the restaurant that morning and when he was told of the birth he told all the customers that his son had a new baby.

There was a beautiful girl about 18 years old whose name I still remember Luce Pilon working as a junior teller at the bank next door who was the daughter of one of our regular customers. Part of her job was to pick up coffee for the staff around 10 a.m. She overheard my father telling some customers about the birth of my new son and she ran back to the bank in tears.

Later that morning when I was back at work the manager of the bank came in for lunch and said that I broke Luce's heart and I asked how and she told me about what my father had been bragging about. I thought Luce had a steady boyfriend so I never paid much attention to her. We all had a good laugh about what happened to poor Luce she was embarrassed to let everyone know about her feelings for me. We dated for some time after that until she moved away.

White slacks and shirt for work and jeans and t- shirts or western shirts and a cowboy hat was my total wardrobe for several years. On the weekends after riding my friends and I would go dancing and have a few beers at the Edgewater hotel or the Maples Inn in Pointe Claire or we would go to Lachine to the El Paso. Life was good.

Lessons learned:

"During this period of my life I improved my cooking skills and love of horses"
I not only learned to cook and run a business but enjoyed what I was doing. Whatever you have a deep interested in something you need to learn more and get better at it

CHAPTER 6

The more things you do, the more you can do.   Lucille Ball

But soon the repetition of doing the same thing work wise became a little boring, and I needed to challenge myself doing something different. One of my customers, Joe Dawson, was a manager for a computer training company who had sales reps calling on leads marketing a key punch program. This was in the early days of computers. He asked if I would be interested in selling a few nights a week. I took the challenge and soon even part time hit the bestseller list just about every other week. When I left high school I did not think that becoming a sales professional was to be my life's career.

Joe had a system of lead distribution which was based on the sales rep with the highest number of sales each week would have first choice of leads in the area he wanted to work the following week.

I being an outgoing friendly sort of guy when entering the sales conference room on Saturday mornings would greet everyone with a good morning or hello! There was one sales rep who never responded. My philosophy was and still is today that if I said hello to you on three occasions and you did not have the decency to respond, I would never say hello to you again; I still do the same even today. Life is too short to deal with idiots.

I found a way through my sick sense of humor to deal with this individual each week thereafter. Joe had a system where you recorded the number of sales beside your name on a board with a sliding tab for each sale. So what I did was I would get up and register 1 or 2 sales and sit back down shuffling my papers and wait until this unfriendly sales rep listed all his sales for the week. Then I would get up once again and add 1 more sale. Remember the sales rep with the most sales for the week got his choice of the best area to work and. I kept adding 1 sale at a time until my number was higher than his and this happened at least twice a month…boy was he pissed and I laughed to myself.

Joe Dawson knew what I was doing, and we became close friends over the years that followed, and in future years, our roles switched and I became his sales manager.

I was learning that my forte and future was to be in sales and marketing, and I started to read books on sales, sales management and leadership and attend sales seminars. The result was that over the following several years I became a sales professional.

I remember a sales training program that I registered for; it was called "Hot Button Selling" conducted by Jack Lacey. He had 1 tear sheet with a ladder drawn on it and at each step was a question. Each question got you closer to the top which was the prospect's"Hot Button". I fully did not understand the concept then, but as I developed my sales skills and later sales training programs, it sure helped.

Attending sales and motivation seminars and listening to audio tapes I found a lot of the content not to meaningful, it was more sizzle than steak. I was able to extract ideas and techniques that I benefited from later in my sales career. Many of the speakers content was what happened in their sales careers in their past life I felt that my sales skills had more substance as I was living it and improving it every day.

Lessons learned:

I learned that selling was one of my strong points and that I was naturally good at it and if this was to be my chosen career I had to learn to be better at it.

CHAPTER 7

Life is always about making choices, always do your best to make the right ones and always do your best to learn from the wrong ones.

After 9 years in the restaurant I felt it was time to move on to other challenges and I responded to an ad for distributors representing a company that was manufacturing stone facing that could be applied to any surface interior and exterior. So I paid a fee to become the exclusive distributor for the Province of Quebec. I felt with the sales experience that I had acquired to date that selling stone facing would be no different than any other product that was sold directly to the consumer. Boy was I wrong because I not only had to sell the product but had to arrange for crews to install it as well, so we became a renovation company. I called the company Miad Stone.

When a home owner wanted to beautify his home he not only wanted to dress up the front of his home but redo the whole exterior. We then added a line of aluminum siding then awnings, aluminum doors and windows and anything that had to do with repairing the exterior of homes. We became a multi task renovation company in our first year of business.

This became a big challenge not only selling but having to supervise our installation crews. A friend of mine joined me and ran the office and did the accounting, we hired a construction supervisor to police the jobs and make sure the customers were satisfied and happy. We arranged financing through one of the top finance companies and needed approvals before commencing work and a signed completion form from the client that all work had been completed satisfactorily before we would receive payment for the work done.

I looked after sales and advertising and training of sales reps and in the first year in business we achieved sales of almost half a million dollars.

The sale of aluminum siding started to attract many pressure sales types and the business became very competitive, some selling for whatever the market would bear. We maintained a per square foot price of $1.25 others were either practically giving it away or gouging the buyer with as much as $2.00 or more per foot .This was known as selling on a par deal. They would then try and peddle their contracts to different companies. We refused any business from these con artists. Some contracts were sold by these par deal con artists to more than one company and some contracts were in fact false sold to non existing home owners or grave yards and empty lots. The companies who bought these contracts soon lost their credibility and even their businesses.

Then came another major problem I heard from some of my suppliers that the mafia or some thugs started visiting many of the smaller companies and were demanding protection money each week or they would be put out of business. I first thought that this was some kind of sick joke, until I visited my awning supplier to check on a few orders. On the way into his shop I came face to face with 5 big burly tough guys just leaving, First I thought nothing of it but when I met one of the owners he asked if I saw the 5 guys who just left. I answered yes and he told me they were mafia and had demanded $150 per week protection money or they would burn his business down. He was as white as a sheet and shaking with fear. He told me that they were after many of the renovation companies for protection money.

That night I hardly slept thinking about what I just experienced and decided that I was not going to be threatened into paying any protection money ,so the next morning I brought my 30-30 rifle to my office prepared to protect myself and my company from these thugs. It became extremely difficult to operate a business under the fear of becoming another victim and having to spend the rest of my life working and paying protection money. What a scary position to be in after starting a new business and working my butt off for over 1 year. Sometimes you make the right decisions but unforeseen obstacles get in your way that you have no control over and sometimes it's best to move on.

Lessons learned:

Not all was a waste because   I had improved my sales and marketing skills and learned how to hire and train sales agents"

Chapter 8

Everything happens for a reason.

A few months before the threat by the mafia the business was doing well and my friends who were mostly married by that time started bugging me that it was time for me to settle down. I was happy in my bachelorhood but agreed to meet the daughter of a well known doctor in Montreal who was living and working in New York. I thought here was an independent lady that maybe I should meet. My friend Bernie's fiancée Sheila arranged the introduction a few weeks later. We met and started seeing each other and too soon I was pushed into becoming engaged.
A week before the wedding we were having dinner at my future in-laws and as we sat down to eat, three armed thugs appeared in the dining room with guns drawn. I first thought it must be some kind of joke or friends who had set up a stag party and had come to pick me up. One of the thugs the leader put a set of handcuffs on my right wrist and told me to lay down on the floor so he could put the cuffs on both hands. At the same time the other two moved to the other side of the dining room table and ordered my future father in law to also lie down on the floor. I moved to his end of the table and turned toward my assaulter who pointed his gun at me and told me to tell my father in-law to lie down or he would shoot him. I grabbed for the gun and while trying to wrestle it free from his hand he kept smashing it against the side of my left ear I managed to pull it out of his hand and it fell and slipped under the window drapes.
   The other two thugs thought the tables had turned and immediately ran back down the basement stairs, leaving me wrestling with the leader. My assailant made a dash for the basement stairs with me in hot pursuit. My fiancé ran to call the police using a phone that was located on a window sill at the head of the basement stairs. As I tried to grab the leader he pulled my fiancé between us and with his back to the stairs I pushed him and down the stairs he went head over heal smashing into the wet bar at the bottom. He quickly got up and ran out the basement door. The police arrived and the detective asked me to get in the car with him and give him a description of the men. I told him that they were armed and that two of them had nylon stockings on their faces but the leader had a scarf covering his face that fell off as we fought. The detective immediately got on his

radio and told the other officers that they were armed and to shoot first and ask questions later. A visit to the hospital to fix my ear and remove the handcuffs still attached to my right wrist and then back for dinner.

A few weeks later when we were on our honeymoon I read about the Santa Clause holdup that took the lives of two Outremont police officers during a bank holdup at the CIBC bank at 6011 Cote de Liesse.. One of the detectives told me they had three suspects in custody and I asked to see some photos. What caught my interest was that one of them was being held in a hospital paralyzed because of a back injury..I wondered if it could have happened to the leader who fell down the stairs and hit his back on the wet bar. I asked my father in-law who was a doctor if someone could become paralyzed a week or two after an injury and his said it was possible. Guess what… the injured suspect was in fact the leader who I fought with and they were the thugs who were charged with the bank hold-up. So much for a little excitement in life, to this day I still wonder what I would have done if the gun had not dropped behind the curtain I remember his name was George Marcotte and another Jules Reeves and the officers killed in the bank hold-up were Claude Marineau and Denis Brabault.

George Marcotte was tried and convicted in killing one of the officers and was sentenced to death but later reduced to life imprisonment and in 1981 was paroled. Remember I had built my wall of protection around me but I made the mistake of opening it a little without first learning to become good friends. Later in life I discovered that for a marriage to work you first need to become best friends then you must be honest with each other and most important you must trust each other 100%.

Well our marriage was not built on any of these as I found out shortly after our marriage that my wife was not only living and working in N.Y. but was involved in a live in relationship. I also found out that she had become pregnant when she was 15 years old and had an abortion. So my wall of protection was back up once again. The marriage was doomed to fail and fail it did. The only thing that kept us together for what I see now was the birth of a beautiful son.

When I look back now here I was the guy from the wrong side of the tracks in a relationship with the upper class and who probably thought that I was not good enough as I did not have the same education or wealth that they did. They were born again Jews and I an atheist, not a good mix.

They tried to convert me to their way of life but that was not who I was, so we had problems from the start. My feelings for them were not much different
The main reason I stayed with the marriage was because of my son when I look back now for not a good decision wasting 19 good years of my life.
I have met many couples that are miserable living with each other but choose to remain in the relationship for all the wrong reasons, what a waste of a life.
Shortly after we married I closed my business as I had a fear of having to potentially deal with thugs or the mafia. Sometimes we get into the wrong situations and we feel that we should give it more time and maybe it will get better. In personal and business relationships I learned that it just doesn't happen. Don't waste good effort beating a dead horse.

Lessons learned:

What did I learn here? Become best friends before taking the leap and be honest with each other. Trust and honesty is essential for a marriage or business relationship to work.

CHAPTER 9

Failure is simply a learning opportunity.

So on to the next challenge in the school of hard knocks. Newly married and with a business that I had just closed it was time to decide once again how I was to support my family. My father in-law arranged a family gathering with two of his brother in-laws who were in the scrap metal and waste paper business and I was fed a lot of crap on now that we were family I should go and work for them. I stated that I was not interested in working for anyone at that point in my life as I had had the freedom of working for myself. Both uncles then said if I went out on my own they would pay me whatever they received from the mills and they would keep no profits, me now being part of the family.

At this point in life I had not yet learned that most people family or otherwise look after themselves first and foremost.

So I bought a truck and formed a corporation called Universal Waste and off I went into a business that I knew nothing about. Any metal I was able to pick up was taken to uncle Harry and any waste paper to uncle Benny and I took them on their word that I would be paid whatever they received from the mills….boy was I wrong, I worked my ass off and secured a large number of accounts such as paper converters, printers, Redpath sugar, Kraft foods etc. and thought I was being paid what was promised. I weighed 135 lbs. and was moving and handling bales of paper weighing up to 1,000 lbs. all by myself.

One day on delivering a load of paper to Kruger Mills I asked the guy on the scale that I had become friendly with what price per ton was Uncle Benny was being paid and he told me $120 a ton. Guess what I was receiving doing all the hard work and after being promised to be paid whatever the mill price was. I was paid a measly $ 30 dollars per ton. Boy was I pissed!

Here I was in my twenties and I had not yet realized that most people are themselves first and maybe you later. Sometimes it's harder to accept greed from family than in a business relationship. I always believed that every relationship has to be based on honesty and trust.

That night I went to see my in-laws and told them what I thought of their family and their promises. I had a choice to make get out of the business or find a broker who I could partner with who was honest.

 I found one based in Toronto and we agreed to partner. I would look the daily operations and he financing the purchase of equipment such as presses to bale the different types of paper and dealing with the various mills. We rented a warehouse from Imperial Tabacco in Ville Lasalle that had its own rail dock and ramp and was over 500 ft. long. Plenty of space to grow the business. At the beginning my main responsibility was to secure new clients which I did and I came up with an idea to put them under contract guaranteeing them a price per ton for one full year and adjusted annually. This was a first in the waste paper business.

 Our business started to boom and we needed additional baling presses. My partner was responsible to finance and purchase these and he researched different sources. The price for manufactured equipment that we needed at the time was over $ 40,000 dollars per press. My partner found a manufacturer that built garbage trucks and claimed he could produce quickly what we needed using hydraulics in place of chain driven presses which were standard at the time. Instead of $ 40,000 for each press we would get two for the same money, it looked like a bargain and they promised quick delivery and a guarantee that they would fulfill our needs. We soon found out there is no such thing as a bargain and dealing with a small manufacturing plant they did not keep their commitment on delivery dates.

In the meantime we were receiving tons and tons of paper each and every day and did not have the equipment to handle it. We worked literally 24 hours a day and still could not keep up. We had a warehouse full of paper and were filling rail cars and the loading ramp stacked to capacity. The delivery of our new presses was scheduled for 30 days from the signing of the order. This date came and went for 4 months and when the presses were finally delivered they did not work and in fact one caught fire and almost burnt down the building and all its contents. It would have been a huge wiener roast. While we were waiting for the new presses I purchased a truck scale from the city of Montreal and had it installed so we could weigh loads coming in. When some of the other scrap dealers got wind of it they offered to pay me cash under the table to reduce the weight of their loads.

So here we were me working 18-24 hours a day and seeing no light at the end of the tunnel all because we tried to save some money on needed equipment. I decided I had enough and told my partner the business was now his and closed the shop and went home exhausted and burnt out from all the stress and work.

Lessons learned:

Chock-up another learning experience!" Beware of family promises as everyone looks after themselves first." Success breeds greed and greed stupidity.

CHAPTER 10

Forget your failures just learn from them

A few nights after I walked away from the waste paper business I saw an ad under sales agents wanted for a representative to market home study courses for an organization called Famous Artists Schools based out of Westport Connecticut. It caught my curiosity and I made an appointment with the regional manager. His name was Larry Hughes and we met the next day. After a brief interview I was hired and he gave me a brochure to read and said that we would meet the next afternoon and make some appointments. I figured he would train me on the procedures and presentation.

 Well the training consisted of driving around to try and set up an appointment for a presentation. I was told to go and talk with the prospect and book the appointment for later that evening. After several stops I was able to book one appointment for that night and I figured that Larry would do the presentation as I knew squat about the programs offered.

When we arrived for the appointment Larry handed me a presentation binder and told me to present. I started to sweat but decided to go ahead anyway, just reading the print on each page, and to my surprise the prospect decided to enroll. Now came the paperwork which I asked Larry to complete. We left that home and Larry handed me the presentation binder and a hand full of leads and that was the extent of my training.

This was my first sale and I made a commission of $135 dollars for an hour of work. Most people were earning that amount for a week's work. I said to myself I can do this and enjoy this type of work. I had graduated back into the direct selling business. If you remember when I was in High School I sold Baby Butler feeding tables direct to the consumer that was Direct Selling and later sold keypunch programs and then home renovations So here I was no training and left to sink or swim all by myself. I was not about to sink so I jumped right in and started making cold calls to book appointments, using what sales knowledge I had acquired in my life to date helped.

Famous Artists Schools had three separate schools teaching writing, art programs and a photography school. Each school had separate sales agents specializing in marketing their programs. Leads were supplied free of charge and there was a no telephone rule to book appointments, you had to cold call door to door to book appointments. At the time I did not fully understand why but agreed to follow the system. I was assigned to market writing programs and for a guy that basically could not even spell the word I thought this should be interesting.

I can recall my first presentation which was on Sherbrooke St. west to two spinster sisters one of which wanted to learn how to write. Before the presentation I asked her some questions on what prompted her to write to the school for information. These few questions became the foundation for a questionnaire that I refined over the years and was the basis for a presentation sequence that I developed and was later used by the sales forces of all the schools.

At the end of my presentation the sisters said that my explanation of the program was the most professional they had ever experienced and asked me how long I had been representing the school. I looked at my watch and almost said a few hours and smiled inside and thanked them. Boy! Did this ever help my confidence?

After selling for a few months I made the bestseller list and was noticed and recognized by top management. I was invited down to Westport Connecticut to meet the Director of the school Norman Carol and given a tour of how exams were graded and what help was available to the students. Boy was I impressed! I also visited the other schools and met some of the Directors who in later years became friends and working associates. I still have photos of that meeting.

When I came back to Montreal some of my friends when we met asked me what I was doing and I said I worked for Famous Artists Schools marketing home study programs. I could tell from their reactions that they were not impressed. From that point on I would say that I worked for Norman Rockwell who was a part owner with other famous artists and that impressed them. So much for stupidity!.

At the beginning I had no idea who our target market was and none of the reasons why someone would want to learn to write and why through a home study program. The school offered a free aptitude test which about 10% of people completed. So 10% of the leads we received were tests and the balance where people who inquired but for whatever reason did not send in a test. I thought and so did all other agents that these were the people most interested and we of course would contact them first for an appointment. The other leads we worked when we ran out of test leads.

Who would you think was our prime market? Men or women? What age demographic?

Whatever I and the other agents thought was totally wrong, even top management had it figured wrong as well. Here's what I discovered! Women, empty nesters ages 45-55 were our prime market. Why? After spending a lifetime bringing up their children they lost touch with the real world forgot how to communicate and needed to learn how to express themselves and communicate through the written word in the privacy of their own homes. Another interesting point was that many of these women were not happy in their relationship with their husbands and were either in the process of separation or divorce and needed to rebuild their confidence. At one point I wondered if anyone remained married after age 45. Now men were different they thought that they had a story to tell, that they had a book within them. The only problem was that they were in the prime of their careers and had inquired with the future intent of learning to write when they retired. The highest percentage of aptitude tests came from men and the lowest number of enrollments, Interesting!

I quickly realized that I can do this and this was the kind of career I was good at and was what I wanted to do. It gave me the freedom to work my own hours and determine my income and earn in one hour what most people earned in a week.

Lessons learned:

What did I learn in my experience as a sales agent with Famous Schools? I improved my sales skills and developed some techniques and tools that were the basis of a future sales and marketing program that I developed and wrote and even sold.

CHAPTER 11

The only place that success comes before work is in the dictionary.

My brother in-law was working as a non licensed pharmacist at the time but requirements changed, and he would have had to go back to university and earn his degree if he were to continue working in that field. I arranged for him to meet the regional manager Larry Hughes to see if he could be hired. With my recommendation, Larry hired him and now he became a sales agent.

 My brother in-law is probably one of the nicest guys you could ever meet, a family man devoted to his children, a good and generous loving husband with only one character flaw….if you said white he would argue that it was black, and because of this flaw, he was a difficult guy to teach as he would argue or find ways to disagree with just about everything you would say. I later learned that he was color blind even though he was a great artist. He could copy any painting and only needed my sister's help in choosing some colors of paint.

So, off he was into a new career in Direct Sales. We would meet every Saturday morning for breakfast at a restaurant in Rockland shopping center for a kosher breakfast of bacon and eggs and compare our weekly results. So maybe it wasn't kosher, but it was delicious. During breakfast, he would ask how many appointments I had that week, and I would take out my pocket agenda and have him keep count….Mon. 2, Tues 3, Wed. 1, Thurs 3, and Fri. 2. I would then ask him how many that was and put my agenda back in my pocket and keep on eating…he would answer 11 appointments. ..I would keep eating, then he would ask how many sales, and I would say why didn't you ask me that when I had my agenda out, and we would repeat the process.. Mon. 1, etc…total for the week 8 sales times $135 which earned me $1080 dollars. He never asked how I was able to book 11 or more appointments, so I never told him. Then I would ask him how many appointments he had that week, and he would answer 3. I never asked how many sales as I could figure that for myself. I also knew that for him to be willing to learn he had to ask and be ready to learn and not argue. This exercise went on week after week for many months.

I knew that he had received the same amount of leads as I did but was not getting the same amount of appointments and therefore not the same amount of sales. After my sister complained to me that he was not making a living, I told her that I would sit down with them on one condition that they would listen and not argue and do what I showed them or go find another career; they agreed. We spent the evening sorting his leads, and I set up a work plan for the week where he would start his appointments on Sunday night on the south shore of Montreal and keep booking appointments through the eastern townships all week and that we would meet in Sherbrooke, Quebec on Friday afternoon and compare notes and results.

 We met at the Le Baron Motel over a beer to review his week's results. He then pulled a reverse on me playing the same game that I had played on him months before. When I asked how many appointments he had booked, he replied he didn't remember. When I asked how many sales he replied a few so I leaned over and opened his jacket and he had a bunch of agreements for a total of 13 sales. He never looked back and became one of the top sales agents. Certain people need to learn the hard way.

As direct sales now became my chosen career, I also needed to learn more and for the first time I saw the inside of McGill University not to become a doctor or lawyer but to learn about sales management as this was my next goal. I registered for a course, and we were about 15 sales managers and me a sales manager yet to be. The course was presented by a professor who I'm sure never sold anything in his life or managed any sales people. One of the exercises was having one of the participants present a management problem he was having. A newly appointed sales manager from Moore Business forms presented his problem for the class to offer suggestions. His problem was that he had decided to realign territories and took his top agent's territory which was Place des Armes office buildings and gave it to another agent. The top agent was furious and was ready to quit. He asked the group for their opinions, and the answers were as bad as the course and professor. When I was asked what I would do in such a situation my answer was to give him Place Desjardins and $ 200.00 dollars and let him pass go.

You should never de-motivate your top agent but reward him and encourage and teach him to increase his production.
So much for formal learning, so back to the school of hard knocks I went to learn by trial and error and by learning to use simple common sense.

In certain areas, Famous Artists at the time did not produce enough leads in the Art and Photo schools to warrant hiring an agent. The Maritime Provinces was one area and was also too expensive to manage from Montreal, so I and other agents were asked to travel and work the leads that accumulated over a few months. Some of the agents who had been around longer were first to travel to New Brunswick.

Their sales results were dismal and after a few trips refused to go again. So as last man in I was asked to go.

I remember my first trip. I decided to start in Campbellford and work my way around to Edmundston and then back home working the leads I had. I arrived there Saturday morning and stopped for breakfast and called my manager Larry Hughes with my weekly sales report. When I told him where I was, he said that another agent was in the next town and on his way back to Montreal and that I would probably pass him on that two-lane highway.
Sure enough he passed me, and I turned my car around and honked my horn to get his attention; he just kept on driving ignoring the blasts of my horn; he must have been daydreaming. I was finally able to pull up alongside him and after rolling down my window and honking some more get his attention, we pulled into a church parking lot, and I asked him how his sales trip went and how long he had been in New Brunswick. He said he was there for a little over a week, and his next comment was that the prospects in New Brunswick were poverty stricken and stupid and that that he made no sales. I asked how many leads he had and then told him I had just spoken to our manager and that he should give them to me to work. This was a little lie, but I figured as he was returning to Montreal that they would go to waste anyway.

Two weeks later after returning to Montreal, we had a breakfast sales meeting, and the agent that I had met on my trip into New Brunswick asked me how my trip went and if I had made any sales. I told him that I had made 23 sales and that 12 of them were from the leads he gave me.

He asked how I could have sold these poverty stricken prospects, and my answer to him was ATTITUDE, my attitude. I told him that I felt that people no matter where they lived had the same desires and ambitions and that I treated them no differently than anyone else. He told me that he had made appointments and when arriving at their home that he would look at what he called a shack and decided it was a waste of time as they probably could not afford the course and off he drove. I upon arriving at the same home took a different view. I looked up at the roof and saw a T.V. antenna and then looked at the cars in the driveway and the 2 snowmobiles parked beside the house and said to myself that these people were buyers and if the interest was there could afford our program and boy was I ever right. What I had learned was to never prejudge or assume, as A.S.S.U.M.E. only means and spells, makes "an ass out of you and me".

Everyone has different priorities and therefore you need to identify what motivates them and that means identifying their "Hot Button".

Lessons learned:

What I learned on these trips. Never assume, never prejudge and treat everyone the same.

CHAPTER 12

Get stronger with each new learning experience.

I became one of the top agents for famous Artists Schools and felt comfortable in what I was doing to earn a living. But I was approached by my then father-in-law's brother also a Dr. who with a group of partners opened a senior citizens home on Bois de Boulogne near Boulevard de L'Acadie in Montreal They had been operating for about a year and were losing money each month. Because of my restaurant experience, he asked me to spend some time at the home and see if I could suggest some improvements.
I observed for a few days and then made my recommendations and a week later was asked to move into one of the empty apartments rent free and oversee the business for which I was to be paid $ 150.00 per week, free food and 8% of all increased revenues paid each quarter. I told him I was happy in what I was doing and did not want to give it up. He agreed that I could continue selling and manage the home at the same time. The offer sounded too good to pass up so in I moved. I must have been a glutton for punishment as I had no desire to work with or for relatives or family ever again. But when I saw to poor conditions these elderly were living I was determined to improve their quality of life.
The facility offered limited nursing care and food that was prepared in a small apartment on the main floor and sent up to the tenants on carts at meal time. Groceries and meats were purchased at retail in local grocery stores as well as all other supplies. The food was prepared by a woman who thought she was a cook using a small apartment stove.
 Vegetables and meat were jammed into small fridges that rotted within a few days. Food trays would be served at meal time and I noticed that very little was being eaten and that the portions were way too large for the seniors to be able to eat. As well the food had no taste.

The first thing I did was purchase a commercial stove and a commercial Frigidaire, Then I had a walk in cooler built for fresh fruits and vegetables. I then taught the cook to prepare tasty meals and smaller portions and the food trays came back empty. I also bought everything wholesale and visited the markets every 2-3 days to keep everything fresh. I brought the total cost down to $1. 25 for 3 meals a day per each resident and this included toilet paper.

 After each meal I would visit with the tenants and ask how they enjoyed their meals. They asked who was now cooking and I said I was teaching the cook how to prepare tasty nutritious food. I became their hero. The next thing we hired a full time registered nurse to manage the personal service workers and practical nurses. We had 24 hour care so it was decided that she move into one of the vacant apartments. Now we were a full service senior's home.

 In the first three months I took the business from a loss to making a profit each and every month. Revenues increased and after 4 months I asked for my 8% commission on the increases. I was told I would be paid the next quarter and when that went by and I did not get paid I started to lose faith in the agreed deal.

 I spoke to my father-in-law and expressed my concerns and he said if my brother said he would pay you then he will. When the last quarter came around I again asked for my commission and was once more ignored I packed up and left without notice. The business reversed to its original state and within a few months was again in the red. I was asked how I had made it profitable and I told them when I get paid I will tell them. I never got paid so they never found my secrets. I once again learned never to trust family in business as they were mostly out for themselves.

Sometimes opportunities seem like a good deal but it's not necessarily so.
While I was managing the senior's home my friend and previous sales manager Joe Dawson dropped by one day and asked me to come with him on a presentation for a new financial service he had just started to sell. He knew that I was selling for Famous Artists Schools and had become one of the top agents. I agreed to go with him on his presentation and in 40 minutes he sold a family a plan to save for their children's post-secondary education. And made $300.00 in commissions.

 He wanted to introduce me to his manager and that I should start selling this new service. I told him that I did not have any time as I was now back selling full time for Famous Artists.

 Joe convinced me to meet his manager. I agreed and thought that this was something my father could do as he was working too hard in the restaurant for the amount of money he was making.

I was hired, and given a presentation manual and some leads and that was the extent of my training. I put the kit in the trunk of my car and forgot about it for a few weeks.

A few weeks later I convinced my father to ride along with me on a few appointments I had made in the eastern townships for Famous Artists Schools. I did two presentations and made both sales and earned $270.00 in about 4 hours which included driving.

 On the way back to Montreal I remembered that I had the kit for the education saving plan in the trunk and stopped on the side of the road and took it out. I asked my father to drive while I read it. When we got to the Champlain Bridge I used the pay phone and made an appointment for about an hour later. I left my father in the car and went and did a presentation and sold 6 units and made another $300.00 dollars. Not bad for a day's work I had earned $ 570.00. The savings plan was called University Scholarships of Canada. So now I was selling two programs and making a good living but I was working 80 hours a week and was on both companies best sellers lists.

A few months later I was interviewed for a possible regional manager's position with Famous Schools by the Canadian president Jim Aird. We had dinner and a few drinks and for a month I heard nothing further, so I assumed I would not be promoted. Then on a Sunday night about 10 pm Jim called and said the position was mine if I wanted it but that I would have to be in Toronto the next morning to be introduced to the sales agents. As a manager I would be paid a salary and an override commission on all sales in Ontario and Manitoba. It would mean earning less for a period until I could increase sales. But as I ultimately wanted to be in a management and leadership position so I decided why not take this opportunity. The next morning I was in Toronto and when introduced to the other agents I saw that I was by far the youngest. The top producers sat at the end of the conference table with negative looks on their faces and in their attitudes all thinking they should have been offered the position. I had to win their confidence and loyalty and this was not an easy task for me as a new regional manager without experience.

I had developed a questionnaire that I used before my presentations and a system of steps that I followed with each presentation as well as a telephone script for making and qualifying appointments. I decided to perfect it over the next few weeks and then start retraining the agents on how they by following it would

potentially increase their sales. The top sales agents were not impressed claiming they needed no help as they said they knew more about sales then I did. So I told them to keep doing what they were doing and asked if anyone wanted to work closely with me over the following weeks and learn my system. One agent stated he would like to try and I taught him my system and went out on field calls with him. The result over the next month was that he outsold the top producers. At our sales meeting some of the other agents asked him what happened and he told them that he was using my system and it worked. From that point all agents were retrained and used my system and increased sales masking me some nice override commissions. This was the first crack at learning to leverage my time and make money while I slept and from that point on I never worked for only a salary.
All of the agents that were hired before my appointment were male so when I started to recruit I made sure the ad read male/female agents wanted. I hired some very strong sales women who after a short while were either matching sales with the men or out producing them. This was noticed by the company President Chuck Miller and he ordered all managers to start hiring more women.

My old manager Larry Hughes refused and I was ordered by Chuck Miller to work with Larry and make certain that he hired some women agents. We placed some ads and I sat in on Larry's interviews and what an experience it was. Larry's first statement to the women who came in for an interview was " I do not believe women should be in sales I think there are two places that they should, be one is the bedroom and the other is in the kitchen." Most women left insulted but a few told him where to go and how to get there. We hired those women and they became top producers. If anyone were to repeat his statements today they would be charged with verbal harassment and fired as regional managers. Larry became a believer and we laughed about his method in later years.
This was another transitional period in my career where I was able to improve my sales and marketing skills. The results of this learning experience carried me into the next phase of my business and personal life.

Lessons learned:

Think outside the box and keep improving your skills.

Chapter 13

In teaching others we teach ourselves.

One year after I was appointed regional manager covering all of Ontario and Manitoba, the North American president of FAS, Chuck Miller, called and promoted me to work in a larger region in the U.S.A. So I applied for my green card and was immediately transferred to Minnesota and Wisconsin. I thought I would feel uncomfortable working in the States but the Midwest was to me similar to western Canada, a little faster pace and just as cold as Winnipeg. I was assigned under a divisional manager named Lee Curtis who was from the south, and he was not in favor of having some Canadian who was friendly with the company President in his territory. Lee was short in height and as I was to find out power hungry and ruled his managers with fear and abuse.

This was my first experience with short bureaucratic idiots in the corporate world. I was to meet and work with many others over the years. I remember one of the other managers who was over 6ft. tall calling in his report shaking in fear and sweating while reporting to Lee. He dared not treat me that same way as he was afraid I would report to Chuck Miller. We did not see eye to eye, and I was happy when several months later Chuck called and said I was being transferred to London. I said to him "been there, done that in Ontario "; he said not that London stupid the other one and corporate wants you there this weekend. I asked why and he said that they had opened a school in England the previous year and were losing their shirts and they needed a training manager and two other training assistants to try and turn things around and I being a Canadian would be accepted over an American. I chose one of my top Canadian agents Archie Dixon and Chuck Miller chose one from the states; his name was Earl Grundstad, someone I had never met.

 So off I went into the wild blue yonder to jolly old England. I was starting to see the world on someone else's expense account. I boarded a flight in Minneapolis that was to stop in Chicago and then on to London. I was told that Earl Grundstad was to board there. Archie was also to join us but took a direct flight from Toronto landing around the same time in London.

When I boarded in Minneapolis, I was seated next to a gentleman from England that worked for Monsanto and had just attended a seminar in St. Paul. When we arrived in Chicago, I suggested we de-board and stretch our legs, and I would try and see if I could pick out Earl from the waiting passengers. I searched every face and could not determine who it could be, so we re-boarded and then watched as the other passengers boarded. Again, I could not determine which one was Earl. The plane was just about full when a young pregnant Italian woman and her European looking husband laden down with carryon luggage passed my seat. I asked if he was Earl Grundstad, and he replied that he was. He asked who I was, and I replied F.B.I. and that after the plane took off I needed to ask him some questions. My flight companion broke out in laughter and all night long Earl kept wondering why the F.B.I. was interested in him. I found out he was taking his wife to Italy to be with her parents while he was on assignment to work in London. I pretended to take notes as I questioned him where he lived and worked which made things funnier. Earl did not sleep a wink that night.

When we landed the next morning, we were greeted by the "Governor "or should I say the CEO from the London office, holding up a sign with our names. I let Earl and Archie introduce themselves first and held back a few minutes then walked up and said who I was; the look on Earl's face was worth my not sleeping all night. We had flown all night as we were told it was important we be there Saturday morning. We were loaded into a chauffeured limo and taken to our hotel. The Governor then told us he had arranged a sales meeting and training session for Tuesday, and we should enjoy our weekend including Monday which was a bank holiday. We all looked at each other and shook our heads in disbelief.

Now that we had a long weekend in front of us, we became tourists and visited some of London's tourist sites including Soho and found some good restaurants and took in a show or two. Archie was a pretty straight type of guy who had never ventured into a strip club and probably never drank more than one glass of wine a month, but over the long weekend that changed somewhat. One night after a few bottles of wine and dinner, we walked through Soho, and as we passed numerous strip clubs, Archie decided it was time for him investigate the workings of a strip club. Earl and I waited outside watching the crowds and hookers go by for almost 1 hour while Archie educated himself.

 By Tuesday, we were ready to start work and made our way to the hotel where the training session was to take place. When we walked in, I was surprised to see a room filled with 60 retired head masters (or what we know as teachers), not a salesman in the group and not one woman. The "Governor" and 2 regional managers sat at the head of the table, and we sat on the side as observers. It was the worst sales training we had ever seen, and both Earl and Archie were ready to jump in and take over, but I told them to cool it and observe.

By noon, even I could not stand it anymore and told the Governor that I would take over the afternoon session and that I needed a projector as I had a movie of the school in Westport, Connecticut .He told me it would take 3 hours as they had to locate an operator; I said I could operate it but that was a no no in London as projectors came with operators or not at all.

. At that point, the wall slid open, and lunch was a full banquet with a bottle of wine for every 2 agents. The previous week no sales were made, and I wondered how we were going to pay for this extravagant show. I felt like I was at a teacher's retirement party. We finally made it through the day and went back to our hotel frustrated.

I told Archie and Earl to stay cool and for the next week or two, just observe, and we would meet and discuss strategy each weekend. We were all assigned to work with some of the so- called agents, and I was sent to Manchester to work with one agent who had yet to sell anything. I checked into the hotel and waited for him to show, and I waited and waited the whole damn week. He did not have a phone so I or the office could not contact him and I later found out they had mailed him a letter which he only received the following week. By the end of the week, I was well fed and rested and ready to clobber whoever was in charge. Earl and Archie experienced similar situations.

Archie went on several calls with one agent, and finally they were able to put on a presentation with a lady who was very interested in our art program. I had told Archie not to interfere in any presentations but just to observe. The agent or should I say retired school teacher presented, and the woman asked the cost; he told her, and she said she was very interested and would like to enroll, and he said he would be back in the area next week and took leave. Archie was livid, and as they were driving back to the hotel, the agent said "Arch" how did I do? Archie did not answer and then the agent asked if he had done anything wrong, and again Archie did not answer. The agent then asked if he had done anything right, and Archie let fly. Earl had similar experiences.

On Friday night, we all got together to share notes, and we were ready to catch the next plane home. I found out that the Chairman of the Board of the company was coming to London the following week, so I arranged a meeting to discuss how we were to continue working or return to the States. He picked me up at my hotel with a chauffeured Dusseldorf limo and driver, and we went out for dinner. I expressed our frustrations and told him that I did not believe how slipshod the organization was and that I thought we were asked to try and turn things around, not be directed by the "blind" the current management, who knew nothing about our business or sales in general. The man who started Famous Schools was Al Dorne, and when he died, the bookkeeper became the CEO and was now the Chairman of the Board. The name Chairman of The Board originated in medieval times when the most important person sat in a chair higher than the others…thus "Chairman". The board were pieces of wood that made up a table, Hence Chairman of the Board. How's that for words of wisdom?

The "Governor's previous employment was as a manager for Schick razors, a long way from the education business. The agents were being paid per interview not on sales made, and when I questioned the stupidity of this arrangement, I was told this was the way things are done in the U.K. I had a list of some more reasons why the company was in the red and discussed these with the Chairman.

- The company leased 12 small cars which were supplied to some agents at no cost.
- Agents were paid per interview
- No sales training
- No proper recruiting procedures
- Lack of proper administration
- Agents were paid monthly.
- The Governor was supplied with a Rover and the manager's with one model down.

The list went on and at the end of our meeting, we agreed that the Governor and managers would report to us, not us to them, and we would attempt to train them. It was also agreed that we would open a new office and bring in an office administrator to run it. So, now our work began.

What an experience! Working in another part of the world and use the skills I had learned to date and as well develop some new sales tools and perfect my sales training techniques.

Lessons learned:

When opportunity presents itself to improve your skills and learn to become a leader take the leap.

Chapter 14

Action is the foundation to all success   Pablo Picasso

We opened an office in Barkeley Square in London, and the company sent in an office manager from their school in Amsterdam to look after administration. He became my second experience with a power hungry, short in height, bureaucratic idiot. Over the years, I learned to spot them a mile away as they all had the same style of management, "motivation by fear."
I discovered that in the sales area we did not have a sales manual or any training materials, so I had a free hand to develop what we needed. I had to start from scratch. I developed and wrote a sales manual and all supporting forms .I set-up a new commission structure after I found out that agents were paid per interview. When I asked what an interview was, this is what I learned an agent would call on a prospect who had inquired about our programs and at the door ask if they were interested in enrolling and without putting on a presentation would send in an invoice at the end of the month at the rate of 12 shillings for what he considered an interview even though he had made no sales.
When I questioned this stupidity, I was once again told this is how things are done in the U.K. Well not on my watch! I designed a commission plan where the agents were paid a commission of 18 pounds per sale plus bonuses on production up to 24 pounds. I took back most of the cars and cancelled their leases. A few I leased to producing agents and charged them so much against their sales. I had cars parked in Bristol, London and Manchester for use by my trainers and for me when we held recruiting sessions and training in those areas.
The first sales meeting and training we conducted with our super sales force of retired headmasters was an interesting one. Whatever I tried to teach them it was met with this comment from one or the other…"In the U.S.A. you can sell like that or say that but not in the U.K"…. and I was referred to as the blasted American who was attempting to teach the British how to sell. After about one hour of this crap, I decided to get tough. I first told them that I was not a blasted American and that I was a Canadian and as British as they were, and from that point, I was respectfully called a blasted colonial.

I then shocked them all by slamming my palm on the conference table and telling them they were all here under false pretences. The look on their faces was priceless. I then said that they had responded to an ad for sales agents and that they could not even spell the word "sales" let alone perform as such. More shock! I then said unless they were willing to learn how to sell they should leave and that I would hire people who were interested. The room went silent, and now they were ready to listen and learn.

In my past training with agents in Canada and the U.S.A. set in their own ways, I always found one or two who were willing to learn and change, and it was no different here. The first one who put his hand-up was a gentleman who had worked in retail sales and earned 18 pounds per week about $ 44.00 dollars Canadian. He had no car, no telephone at home and his Scottish wife had not been to visit her parents since they were married; as well, they had 2 children. I could not imagine ever having to live like that.

After the training session which lasted 2 days, I worked with him one on one for 2 weeks and went on sales calls with him then cut him loose to work on his own. In his first month after training, he earned 250 pounds and soon the others took notice and began to follow my sales methods, and we now became a sale team. Those retired headmasters that wouldn't adapt were terminated, and new agents were recruited. Sales increased each week. My star agent's commission cheque the second month was 450 pounds, and when he went to his bank to cash it they must have thought that he was a member of the "great train robbery".

The office manager's name was Juergen Persh and now that he was in a position of power played the part to the hilt. He had a British accent and pretended to act like the proper English gentleman although he was far from it. He lived In the best hotel and hired a limo and driver to chauffer him around while I took the "tube" or walked to and from the office..

One evening, I joined him for dinner at his hotel, and he ordered several drinks before dinner, fine wine with dinner and after dinner drinks and an expensive cigar. I was eating at the local pubs or fish and chips or the occasional hamburger at McDonalds. Something was not right here as we both had similar expense accounts.

One night after he had a few too many drinks, I asked him about his background and where he was born, and the truth slipped out. He was born in Brooklyn N.Y. and had some schooling in England and therefore his British accent. He played the part well. He was a total control freak and would have a bird every time one of his staff word talk or spend time in my office. Well, Juergen or no Juergen, I was there to do a job, and a job I did. England was, as I look back, a wonderful experience for me. I was able to develop and prefect my system of training and selling without interference by higher-ups who thought they knew better than I. I grew more in my management development in that period which was a tremendous asset in the years that followed.

Archie and Earl and I worked our butts off during the week recruiting and training new agents all over the U.K., and we would arrive back at our hotel Friday nights. The weekend was our time to relax and enjoy. We ate at the best restaurants and took in the sights and entertainment that London had to offer. I remember one afternoon we went for lunch at what was called the "Elizabethan Room" styled as an old English pub or eating place. The floors were covered in sawdust; there were large wooden tables and "wenches" as waitresses. We sat at a table with 6 other people who were all British. Food was served in large bowls to be shared by everyone at the table. Cheap red wine was served like it was water, and as soon as you took a sip, your glass was refilled. Earl got somewhat smashed and started to act like an typical American idiot, toasting everyone in the place and pinching the "wenches "rear ends. He ended up spilling his cup of wine all over my white shirt and slacks, shocking our reserved English lunch partners at our table.

 I was pissed and had to find a way to get even. Earl had hung his jacket over the back of his chair and had placed his expensive sun glasses in his breast pocket. I decided to take a potato from a bowl on the table and put it in with his glasses and then crush it. Everyone at the table except Earl saw me do this and cheered and laughed. When lunch was over, we walked outside into the bright sunlight, and Earl pulled out his sunglasses which were covered in mashed potatoes. The look on his face was priceless. I ran behind a tree laughing as Earl realized who the culprit was, and things got funnier. As he stepped onto the sidewalk and started to run toward me, he bumped into a young boy eating a hot dog he had just purchased, and the hotdog jumped out of the bun onto the sidewalk. The kid started to cry, and as luck would have it a "Bobby" or as we know it a cop was right there, and Earl had to buy the kid a new hotdog. Archie and I could not stop laughing. So much for childish fun, but what the hell; that's all part of life.

Earl was asked to go to Amsterdam to train some agents for a week and when he came back he brought with him several pornographic magazines which he had strewn around his room. One night after dinner, Archie and I went to his room to plan our next week's activities, and Archie who was in his 50's but had never opened such a magazine picked one up and was in shock, but we could see intrigued. When we left, Earl gave him 4 magazines to read or should I say look at the pictures.

 Two weeks later Archie's wife was coming to London to join him, and when I arrived back in London about midnight and as I was preparing to go to bed, I heard a knock at my door. I opened it, and there was Archie with a brown paper bag in hand. He handed it to me and I said what is this, and he replied it was Earl's magazines and that his wife was arriving in the morning, and he did not want them in his room. The next day when I saw Earl, I gave him back his magazines but we discovered instead of 4 there were 5 magazines…where did the other magazine come from? From that point on, every time Archie and his wife and Earl and I were together, we opened our briefcases and took out a magazine; we would roll it up and try to give it to Archie in front of his wife; he would get red in the face and decline, and Earl and I would laugh…poor Archie coming out late in life!

My training assignment was extended from two months to an indefinite period, and I told the Chairman if I was to stay on he would have to agree to bring my wife and son to London at the Company's expense. It was agreed, and they soon arrived. Having my son there was a wonderful experience for him even though he was only five years old. He recalls that experience even today. Bringing my wife was another matter as I was not happy with our relationship and did not fully trust her ,but that is another story.

One of the executives working in Amsterdam met and fell in love with an airline stewardess, and we decided to throw a bachelor party for him at a dinner club in London called "The Talk of the Town". What a bash we had: a non- ending dinner and a bottle of booze between each 2 guests. We were about 30 including the CEO of Linguaphone School of Languages that Famous Schools had recently purchased and some executives from State side. One who sat directly across from me was Victor Keppler, a famous photographer and partner in our Photography School

 After several hours of fun, food and entertainment the maitre'de brought our bill; by that time it was about a yard long. He asked who was going to settle the account, and I pointed him at Juergen who did not have a company credit card yet. No one else wanted to pick up the tab; Juergen asked the CEO from Linguaphone who said he also did not have a credit card. The maitre'de handed me the tab, and when I looked at the amount, it exceeded my credit limit on my credit card by a mile. Without batting an eyelid, I said to him "my good man can you prepare separate checks". Victor Keppler fell off his chair laughing as there was no way anyone could figure who drank more or who ordered cigars. I then said " my good man add your normal gratuity and mail the bill to Linguaphone School of Languages "and he said "on Regent Street sir "and I said yes, and we all got up and left. I thought we would be arrested the minute we stepped outside, but the bill was received a few days later at Linguaphone's office and the CEO had a bird as this was not his to pay. Famous Schools picked up the tab, and it was a night I will never forget.

In Early August, it was finally decided to terminate the "Governor" and the regional sales managers as they did not understand nor would accept our sales procedures or had in any way attempted to adapt to our training or systems. I was offered the position as National Sales Manager. I said I would accept if they met my conditions. I wanted my salary and overrides to be paid into my U.S.A. bank account, and that I was to receive a living allowance and increased expense account in England. For that I was ready to sign a three year contract. At that time, corporate assigned a new CEO, an American who was working in Amsterdam, to take charge of the U.K. operation. It became his decision to make.

 This was my first experience in understanding the "Peter Principle", a concept that I had heard a little about but had never experienced firsthand. The "Peter Principle" in the corporate world is promoting someone to a level way above his/her capabilities. It's the corporate way of promoting someone all the way up to Chairman and out the back door. The new CEO was, in my opinion, probably 2-3 levels above his capabilities and was unable or afraid to make a decision even if his life depended on it. I waited a month for a decision to my terms and as he kept delaying, I decided to head back to the U.S.A. by the first week of September so my son could start school.

Lessons learned:

 This experience gave me a view into the workings of a poorly run organization and my first understanding of the "Peter Principle".

If you are good at what you do and want to move to a higher position make sure that you first learn the skills that you will need. A good sales agent many times makes a lousy manager.

Chapter 15

Our greatest weakness lies in giving up, the most certain way to succeed is to try one more time. Thomas Edison

Back to the good old U.S.A. I went and when I arrived I went to see Chuck Miller for my next assignment only to discover that my old Divisional manager Lee Curtis was now the new national sales manager and while I was in the U.K. he took the opportunity to spread some untrue things about me and my management skills. He had used the opportunity while I was away to feather his own ambitions and as I found out later had done the same to many others. Chuck was taken in by his lies and appointed him National sales manager. All the other managers and division managers were not happy with his appointment and openly expressed their feeling about his management style to Chuck but he made his decision and was temporarily stuck with it. He did not realize at the time that Lee was his enemy and was after his job as President.
I was ready to resign and head back to Canada, but after Chuck hearing about my successes in the U.K. he convinced me to be assigned under a division manager in the north east who hated lee Curtis more than I did. I was first assigned to take over Connecticut and part of Mass. and we moved to Enfield, Ct. My son started school there and after the first day at school his teacher said it was wonderful to have him in her class. He told her about England and over the next few weeks brought some English coins to show the other students.
Within 6 months I was asked to take over a much larger territory based out of Boston covering Maine, New Hampshire, Vermont, Mass, Rhode Island and parts of northern New York State. We moved to a small town, Milford, Mass. And my son changed schools and adjusted quickly as he seemed to enjoy meeting new teachers and students. Lee Curtis was still national sales manager but I had very little to do with him but at a sales conference he praised my efforts and results and even apologized for his previous mischarges against me. I still did not trust him as he was a "jackal" ready to attack anyone to his own betterment and advancement. A "jackal" in the corporate world is one hides himself in the corporate structure

and when an opportunity arises for him to kill off any competition he "strikes" and moves up the ladder. This was Lee Curtis's style of management.

Working in New England and living close to Boston gave me a deeper sense of what happens in most major US cities, ghettos which as a Canadian I had never experienced. I remember going on a sales call with a new agent in what was called the Blue Hills. When we arrived I thought I was in Westmount in Montreal with beautiful million dollar homes. The prospect told us to call her when we arrived and she would come out to meet us. We called and out she came with a huge German shepherd dog. Her sister joined us for the presentation and sat beside me. When she opened her purse I noticed a handgun. I asked her if she worked for the police force. She said no that it was for their protection.

I did not understand and she said do you know where you are, and I said near Boston and that I was a Canadian and knew very little about the area. She told me that their home was situated close to Dorchester which was Boston's ghetto. At night and sometimes during the day some gangs would try and rob the residents and that's why the dog and gun. What did I know of ghettos and living in fear? When I received a lead report from Westport I noticed that there were thousands of leads in certain postal codes not issued or worked. I asked my agents why and they told me that those codes were in the Ghetto. No sane agent would ever venture into any Ghetto for fear of his life.

I felt that there must be a way and came up with an idea. Why not rent a hotel or motel room close to the Ghetto and invite prospects to come there for a presentation. The first weekend we tried it we made several sales and as I always believed that no matter where you live we all have the same desires, dreams and ambitions. Never judge or prejudge. It became a once a month sales blitz and agents fought over who was to accompany me.

I arrived home late on Friday night and my wife told me Chuck Miller had called and wanted to speak to me. I returned his call and he told me he had terminated employment with Famous Schools and was now the President of International Correspondence Schools in Scranton, Pa. He wanted me as part of his management team but because of his termination agreement with Famous Schools could not offer me a position. I asked who took over as President and boy was I right when he said it was Lee Curtis the "jackal" who had literally stabbed him in the back. He then said if I sent in a letter of termination that night to Famous Schools and flew to Scranton on Sunday for dinner with him I would be working with him starting

Monday morning. After hearing that Lee was to be my new boss I sat down and terminated my employment effective immediately and I mailed a copy to the Chairman of the Board with my reasons for not wanting to be part of an organization who would promote an individual such as Lee to a position as important as President when he was so disliked by the fields managers. I got even at last.

There were a few places that I never thought I would live or work and one was Scranton, Pa. Scranton was originally a coal mining town and ICS "International Correspondence Schools was founded there in the year 1890, when a newspaper editor wrote articles about mine safety because of the many mine accidents that were happening in the area at the time. This became the first correspondence or distance learning school in the world. The school soon became International in scope and offered many different courses and subjects. But as times changed and education requirements changed ICS did not recognize or move with the times and were now in a financial decline and sought out a new team of executives and managers to move into this new era.

Chuck's new team existed of only several of us and when we arrived were considered by the current staff as outsiders who wished we were not hired to disturb their organization which had been around for over 79 years before Chuck Miller and his marketing team .They thought that they were much smarter than us. Initially we were only six and were pitted against 450 home office staff, some who had been with the organization for 40 years or more .The field sales force consisted of another 650 agents and some of them were also around for 40 years as well. So we were up against 1100 of them and only 6 of us.

The sales organization was divided into 5 divisions each headed up by a divisional director. Each division operated autonomously and had different management titles within its structure. An example in the Southern division the management structure was supertendent's, regional managers and sales agents…while in the Eastern division the structure was ; district managers and sales agents. Out west it was again different. There was neither uniformity to the structures nor any one specific national training program.

In the first few weeks I recommended a friend and previous sales agent to fill a position that was open in the southern division as a regional manager his name was Wally Ralston. When he arrived in Atlanta the Divisional director held a sales meeting and for 2 days the discussions centered on the new marketing group,

Chuck Miller an outsider and his group of 5 other outsiders. On the second night Wally called me and said he wanted to quit as he could not work with this bigoted group. I asked him why and he said he would prefer not to say, I insisted he tell me and he said that most of the day was spent talking about me, who they never even met and the discussions were that I was a Jew and the company never hired a Jew in 79 years. I told Wally that these comments did not bother me and gave him a message to deliver to the divisional director the next day and the message was this….a Jew today and next week an afro-American manager and the following week another would be hired and one would be placed in his division, I told Wally to let the divisional director digest that and report his reaction to me. He called that night and said that the group reaction was that they would do whatever it took to get rid of us. As they say "lots of luck". They had no idea who they were up against.

I was soon to discover that ICS employees were all totally anglo- saxon and most belonged to the same church in Scranton. Boy did we have our work cut out for us. I suggested to Chuck that I temporarily act as a regional trouble shooter and go out in the field with some of the existing management and agents and try and get the "lay of the land " and see how they were managed and trained and as well their sales and marketing procedures. As well that I should spend time with the inside staff and feel them out as to their feelings about the new direction we were going to take in the marketing and development of packaged career programs.

I decided to start with the home office staff and was not surprised when I was viewed as an enemy being part of the new marketing team and a Jew to boot.

ICS had its own typesetting staff and prepared mechanicals ready for print as they also had their own print shop on the premises. Chuck asked me to have a form typeset and printed and he needed it that day. I was told that I needed approval from the head of that department a Jack Loftus and was pointed in the direction of his office. The building contained a staff of 450 employees and unless you knew exactly where you were going you could spend half the day wandering the hallways. After asking several people where Mr. Loftus's office was I finally was able to meet him. I introduced myself and told him that I was part of the new marketing team and the new President needed a form typeset and printed he told me I would have to go see the supervisor of the typesetting department which happened to be at the other end of the building. So off I went down the halls again and after about a half hour found the typesetting department. I was passed from one typist to another finally meeting the supervisor and told her that the new president Chuck Miller wanted this form typeset today and printed. She said she could only do it in 2 or 3 weeks. I told her my orders were to have it done today, she replied that I would have to get permission from her boss and when I asked who it was she replied Jack Loftus. Back down the halls I went fuming as I felt that I was being jerked around. When I saw Jack he said that if his supervisor said she could not do it for 2-3 weeks so be it. I then said Jack you have your job to do and I have mine, I am not here as your enemy and either we can work together or I will go out of house and have this form typeset and printed today and whatever the cost it will be charged to your department. I also told him that the new marketing group was here to make the company profitable and protect his and everyone else's jobs and that we would all have to work together to achieve this. The form was typeset and printed within the hour. I established relationships with the supervisors in every department and was accepted as not only a co-worker but friend over the next few months. I was the only one of our marketing team invited to play golf with them and attend their staff parties and barbeques.

I next called the divisional director for the eastern division and told him that I would like to meet with him and then arrange to spend time with one of his district managers. He told me he was too busy and he would have his district manager call me so that we could meet. A few days later we made arrangements to meet for lunch and when I arrived instead of the district manager I was met by one of his agents. We had lunch and then made some sales calls together. Not a bad start snuffed off by the divisional director and his district manager, wrong moves on their part, little did they know that I had worked with idiots before and I learned how to deal with them. I visited another division and was treated the same way. Now I was ready to report back to Chuck Miller and the vice President who name was Lou Robinson. Lou had been with ICS for many years and was now reporting to Chuck and not to happy having his authority and abilities questioned. When I was asked to give my report, Chuck asked what I had discovered and I said you really do not want to know. Chuck said what do you mean! I answered that you are not going to like what I have to report. I said we have two problems to deal with, a sales force that consists of 5 divisions managed by idiots who think and act like they own their own empires. They think that the home office staff are all idiots and that they alone run the company. They were also totally against us as the new marketing team and are prepared to do whatever it takes to have us ousted.

On the other hand you have a staff of 450 employees who think that the mailman is responsible for any business they receive and have no respect for the sales force. Go figure 650 agents against 450 home office staff and us in the middle. Chuck was not a happy camper after my report and asked my opinion what had to be done to turn things around. I told him we would have to rebuild the complete sales force, replace the Divisional Directors if we were to succeed in turning the company around.

We started to recruit sales managers from some of the other home study and resident training schools as well as some of the better managers from Famous Artists Schools and placed them within each of the existing divisions. This caused all kinds of political upheaval and the fun began. In the meantime Chuck Miller hired a new advertising manager and was working 24/7 developing 13 new packaged training programs. ICS up to this point was selling courses that were sold by subject at an average cost of $ 35.00 per subject and when completed by the student the agent would then revisit them to re-enroll for the next subject until the course was complete. This in some cases because of the numbers of subjects would take years and the agent would because of his many visits become like family.

Right around the time we were working on our 13 packaged programs, there was a glut of university students who had just graduated who could not find jobs. The year was 1969 and the U.S. department of education realized the problem and started to promote that students should enter the trades. They produced a booklet to promote this and their key line was …" 11 careers you could learn without a university education"promoting learning a trade.

As we were working on packaging 13 career programs we ordered thousands of these information booklets and designed an advertisement around this booklet introducing our 13 career programs you could learn by home study. These included most of what the government was recommending. When we were ready with our 13 career programs we rolled out our advertising and we received a truckload of inquiries by offering this booklet, it was one of our most successful campaigns.

As we were now ready to start replacing many of the existing field managers and divisional managers even though we were still were a few months away from introducing our packaged career programs, I and a few others who were originally part of the new marketing team assumed we would be the first to be considered for divisional positions when the final structure was decided. But word of our new programs and marketing began to spread to other sales organizations and many of Famous Artists management and they started to apply for some of the management positions .It became a game of politics, who could kiss ass better with Chuck Miller, who ultimately would have the last say in deciding who filled what position. The games were on. This was my second insight to political games that people play in the corporate world.

While all this politicking was going on I was asked to take over a region close to home office and report directly to Chuck. One day when I dropped-in the see how things were progressing with the development of the new programs I discovered that while I was working my butt off in the region, decisions had been made regarding the appointment of the 5 divisional directors and I and another manager who were the first ones to be hired were passed over. I was pissed and was ready to quit and return to Canada. I met with Chuck and told him how disappointed I was and that I had some serious thinking to do over the next few weeks.

 He invited me to lunch and asked that after lunch I review some of the marketing material that was being worked on and to review the sales training manual that was being written. I spent the afternoon reviewing marketing materials that I had been told by Chuck was in its final stages. After I reviewed what was supposed to be a presentation binder I realized that whoever had put it together did not have a clue what was required. I next went looking to find out the status of the sales manual and finally found that it was given to a technical writer to design and write. When I asked to see what had been written he pointed at the door of his office and taped to the back of the door was an outline that was given to him by someone listing what the sales manual was to cover. He looked at me and said I can't even spell the word sales let alone write a sales manual. I asked who gave it to him and was told it was a new guy that was trying to politic his way into becoming the new V.P. of sales.

Chuck had asked me to report back to him with my opinion of what I had reviewed and when I told him what I saw was a load of crap and that no sales manual existed, he did not believe me as he probably thought I was just playing sour grapes.

I left home office that afternoon totally disillusioned and decided to drive back home to Milford, Mass. and think about my future with this company. As I was driving I started to feel a cold or flu coming on and decided to check into a motel and get some R and R and do some thinking. My cold or flu got worse and I spent 3 days at the motel before driving home.

When I arrived home Friday evening I had several messages from Chuck to call him A.S.A.P. When I called him he asked where I was and I replied I was thinking and said this was part of what my job entailed and I was also thinking about my future. He said after I had left his office he investigated what I had told him about the status of the presentation and sales manuals and that I was 100% right and that I should get my ass back to Scranton and help with their design. I told him I had a region to manage and could not do both. He said forget the region that this was more important as the new packaged programs would be ready to go to market in the next 2-3 months and we needed to complete the sales materials in time. So onto my next challenge where I could use my acquired skills that I had learned to date.

Lessons learned:

What did I learn from this experience? That I was good at evaluating situations and people and that to play the game you have to learn to become a somewhat of a Politician.

Chapter 16

Innovation distinguishes between a leader and a follower. Steve Jobs

When I arrived back in Scranton, I was booked into the Sheraton Hotel on a monthly rate with some of the other executives as none of us was prepared to relocate until our final positions were confirmed and secure.
I asked Chuck what he wanted me to work on and he replied first the sales manual and all supporting forms that would be needed to kick-off the new programs and be used to train our new sales force. I smiled to myself as I had written a sales manual when I was in England and could easily adjust it and the other forms that were required without too much effort. Little did I realize that I would have to sell my concepts to not only Chuck but also some of the others who were vying for the sales manager's position and the national training manager's position?
  Chuck had just hired a fellow who had previously been a professional radio broadcaster as a possible to fill the training position; his name was Bob Mudd and even I was impressed with his vocal skills. He could pronounce words with such clarity and some even that I could not spell. I liked the guy, but there was something that bothered me and that I could not put my finger on at the time but it came to me later as I worked with him on some training materials. Remember when I was in high school a popular radio announcer recommended I should consider this as my career.
While I was busy with the writing of the sales manual, Chuck called me into his office and told me he had just discovered that ICS had a packaged Interior Decorating program on the shelf that had been gathering dust for the last 3 years. How he discovered this was that ICS had signed an agreement with an Interior Decorator from New York who had written the program and who was to be paid on a royalty basis per program sold..It was up for renewal, and Chuck did not know what to do. Chuck had heard that very few programs if any were sold and asked me to investigate and report back to him as he had 1 week to decide what to do.
I first had a complete program ordered from stock and then went to see a supervisor from the lead department to inquire about previous advertising and any leads that had been received in the last 3 years. I was told all advertising had stopped the previous year as no sales to her knowledge were made. I asked how

many leads had been received in previous years and was shocked when she gave me the numbers. ICS had received around 15,000 leads over a 2 year period. I asked her to issue about 50 leads in towns close to the Mass. pike and on toward Buffalo, N.Y. I then jumped in my car and drove to the closest town and checked into a motel and opened the box containing the Interior Decorating program. I studied the material that night and in the morning went to the local K-mart and purchased a ruler, exacto knife, binder and some plastic binder sheets. I cut out some of the pages from the program and made a presentation manual and then wrote a questionnaire with a few general questions as a track to use before my presentation.

 Chuck had told me that the program was listed for $ 495.00 which sounded reasonable to me at the time, and I could not figure why no sales were made. I decided to add a few features and benefits to the program to make it more salable and decided on my own to test market it with the new features at $ 695.00. I added business cards, letterheads and envelopes which the student would receive upon graduation together with their diploma identifying them as Interior Decorators which would allow them to purchase furnishings at wholesale.

 I then called the leads I had in that area and tried to make some appointments. The people I spoke with were surprised that I was calling as they said they had inquired 1-3 years prior and either never heard from anyone or that an agent had called but never arranged for a presentation. After some quick thinking, I told them that the reason I was calling was ICS upon reviewing our records had discovered that no reports had been recorded as to call results. I apologized on behalf of ICS and told them my job was to visit with them and explain the program and get their opinions as to its contents and that they were under no obligation to enroll. I booked 2 appointments for the evening and the reception of the program was very positive and I enrolled 1 new student.

From these 2 presentations, I added some more questions to my questionnaire and a few more pages to my presentation and then moved on to the next town and booked another appointment. I sold that one as well; so far, 2 sales out of 3 presentations, not a bad start. I again adjusted the presentation manual and changed some of the questions and continued my trip which now was to towns off the 90 turnpike toward Buffalo.

After 5 days on the road, I had made 8 presentations and had made 6 sales. It was time to return to Scranton and report back to Chuck as to my investigations and results. I not only sold 6 programs but developed a presentation that worked; not a bad week but the most important for me was that I stimulated my creativity which I was going to need over the following months.

When I met with Chuck in his office, he asked how many presentations I was able to make and I answered 8 and then I waited for his next question "did you make any sales?" I first told him that the leads I worked were 2-3 years old and then said I made 1 sale. He said great and I took the agreement out of my pocket together with an initial deposit of $ 250.00; he looked at it and then I handed him another with a deposit of $100.00, and he said fantastic, and I handed him another with a deposit of $ 300.00. I kept pulling out agreements but when I handed him the last one which had a full payment of $ 695.00 he then noticed what he thought was an error and said hey! Wait the program sells for $ 495.00 and I said no! it did not sell for $ 495.00 in fact, no sales were ever made at that price and that I took it upon myself to make changes to the program and I decided to raise the price. He looked at me and then broke out in laughter. The Interior Decorating program became one of our best selling programs and probably still is today.

Chuck had the agreements framed with copies of the deposit cheques and hung them in the conference room for all to see.

Lessons learned:

This trip started my creative juices flowing which I was soon to learn would come in handy in my next position.

I learned is that you have to show initiative, take authority and even if you only are right 50% of the time you're so far ahead of the game.

Chapter 17

There is a way to do it better find it. Thomas Edison

While I was busy writing the sales manual and working on a presentation manual, Chuck and the advertising manager were busy writing and designing fulfillment booklets as part of a mailing that would be made on each of the 13 career programs to prospects who responded to our advertising. Chuck would write something one day and change it the next. This went on week after week, and when one was ready for typesetting and graphics, I was given the task of working with the mechanical department as I had made friends with them and could get things done quickly. Even when the mechanicals were completed, Chuck would review it over and over and make more minor changes. It became a joke on how many times graphics and words had to be changed.

One day when I went up to the mechanical and graphics department, I noticed that one of the graphic designers quickly put in his desk drawer a fulfillment brochure which I thought was for the new High School program. When I asked to see it, he got red in the face and said it was something he had worked on for himself. I insisted that he show it to me and he said o.k. but I was not to tell anyone about it. It was in full color and the cover was an exact duplicate of the high school brochure, but when I opened it, all the pages were filled with porn. After my initial shock, I laughed and said I wanted to take it and play a joke on Chuck when we reviewed changes to other brochures. He panicked thinking he would lose his job, and I promised that I would not reveal who designed it.

 So a few days later when I was with Chuck in his office going over final changes to several brochures, I slipped the high School porn brochure in the pile. After about 2 hours of corrections, he finally came to the High School brochure and checked the copy on the cover and approved it; he opened the brochure, and the expression on his face was priceless. After his initial shock, he angrily said "who is responsible for this porn" and I said I was sworn to secrecy and that he would have to kill me to find out. Finally, he saw the humor, and we laughed and then he said that he wanted to keep it to play the same trick on some of the other managers. So much for my sick sense of humor, but that is what has kept me sane and from becoming a raving alcoholic as many others that I worked with had become. They had no sense of humor and could not take the pressures of the corporate world

On a Sunday night, Chuck and I and several managers after working all day were on our way to dinner and one of the managers took out an audio tape of Don Rickles being roasted by Dean Martin and other top celebrities. It was raw and priceless humor, and we all sat in the car for an hour listening and laughing, almost missing our dinner reservation.

I had heard that Famous Schools had closed its U.K. operation and that everyone working there was fired. Later that week when I was walking down the hall toward Chuck's office, I saw someone walking very slowly, and it appeared that he was either sick or had very little energy. When I passed him, I recognized that it was Juergen Persh who was the office manager in the U.K. for Famous Schools. I asked him what brought him to Scranton, and he replied he was here to apply for a job as he had met Chuck before he was sent to Amsterdam to work. He looked like he had been hit by a truck, and it was pitiful to see a man so broken. He told me he was fired without termination pay and had to pay his own flight back to the U.S.A. Chuck at the time needed a "Joe boy", and he took pity and hired him. So here I was, having to deal with him once again. At first he was o.k. but as time went on and his position became more stable, he went back to his old ways of managing others under him by fear and playing the part of the proper English gentleman which he was far from.

A few more ex- managers from Famous Schools applied for jobs and the games went on. An x-manager from New York who had worked closely with Chuck became part of the woodwork, just hanging around and politicking for the position of national sales manager; his name was Danny Grota, a tough talking guy and another guy who applied for the position of national training director. So now Bob Mudd the x-radio announcer had a competitor. It was an experience for me to witness the games and politics that were being played as well as the ass kissing that went on with Chuck.

As time went by, I started to recognize that neither of the people had the experience or abilities to fill these positions. When I completed my sales manual and some of the supporting sales forms, I arranged to meet with Chuck for final approvals before going to print. When I arrived at his office, there were the two potential national training managers and Danny Grota . Chuck asked me to review my training and sales manual and forms with all of them for their opinion. What a zoo; everyone had their own opinions on what we needed, but none of them was capable of producing any of it. I explained everything in detail and the reasons for each form and sales training sequence, only to be challenged by the others at each step. Chuck did not say a word; he just listened and observed. After several hours of back and forth, I said this program will work, and I needed an approval to go to print or let someone else design what they thought would work better. Chuck just looked at me and said go to print; this is what we need to retrain the sales agents and managers.

A few weeks later, Chuck invited me to have lunch with him, and as we were driving, he told me he was going to announce the appointment of the national training manager that afternoon and asked my opinion about the two candidates he was considering. Over lunch, I gave him my opinions and told him that I did not feel that either one of his choices was capable of doing the job required. He asked who I thought could do the job better and I said that I could but that I was not interested in the position. He asked why, and I replied that the national sales training director would be responsible to train all managers and be paid on a salary basis only while the field managers would be paid a base salary and overrides on all sales made in their regions. I would do the bulk of the work, and they would reap the benefits. I told Chuck that I had always worked on commissions and overrides and would not be interested to work on a salary.

Later that afternoon, Chuck called me to his office and said that I was now the National Training Director and that I should go back to my office and work-up a compensation plan to include an override on sales. That was probably a first time a training director was ever paid an override.

Danny Grota was also passed over for the national sales manager's position, and Chuck hired Gus Becker who had been with Career Schools out of Wisconsin. Gus and I hit it off and worked well together. He was the first manager that I reported to that I learned anything from. He had been the national sales manager with Career Schools and knew and travelled throughout every state in the U.S.A. He was not only sales smart but as well knew every gourmet restaurant in every nook, city or town in every state. So we not only worked well together but we also ate well. Gus was a man of his word and whatever he said you could take to the bank. Just after Gus was hired, we were working on a program with Pan American Airlines for ticket agents, and it was our job to train all the managers in every division on the new program. So, off Gus and I went on our cross country training session. The second to last stop was in Denver,and then onto Los Angeles for our last training session. When we arrived at the airport Friday morning with our confirmed tickets, we were told the flight was overbooked, and we would have to take a later flight which would have gotten us in Los Angeles too late for our training session. As we were frequent fliers and members of American Airlines executive club, we were able to fight our way onto the flight and were seated on jump seats in the first class section. The stewardess came over and told us that she did not have enough breakfast meals on board for us, but she could find us as much cheese and crackers we could eat as well as all the champagne we could drink. Full of cheese and crackers and a few sips or should I say a little champagne we landed in Los Angeles; we both were slightly hung over. I did not think that could happen from eating cheese and crackers, so it must have been the gorgeous stewardess that made my head spin.

When we arrived at the hotel, we gave our bags to the bell captain and told him we would check in after our meeting. As we were both feeling no pain, the training session became one of the most humorous we had conducted to date. Gus would be explaining some things, and I would go to the washroom and when I was covering some other part of the training Gus would head to the same place. When we explained some of the rules of how presentations were to be conducted, it became even funnier. We stated that the agents were not allowed to wear an airline captain's uniform or arrive at the prospect's home with a stewardess on his arm. These were no- no's! And any agent reported doing so would be terminated.

We finally finished the training about 6 p.m., and Gus and I went to retrieve our bags, and as we did I looked at Gus and said are you thinking what I'm thinking and without another word we caught a cab back to the airport and off to Vegas we flew. As we had no reservations, we asked the cab driver to find us a hotel; he looked at me and thought for some reason that I was the actor that played the part of detective Joe Friday whose real name was Jack Webb. Seeing it was Friday, I said I was and we needed a good hotel. We checked in, had a shower and that was the only time we spent in the room that night. I guess after a full week's work we needed some fun time before heading back to Scranton.

Lessons learned:
Work hard.play hard and enjoy what you are doing. Never take life to serious.

Chapter 18

Positive thinking will let you do everything better than negative thinking. Zig Ziglar

Well, after our R and R in Vegas, it was time to head back to the top of the world, Scranton; well maybe not the top of the world, but the airport was situated on top of a mountain with a relatively short runway, and I always envisioned we would fall off the end, either taking off or landing…it was my weekly thrill! As the airport in Scranton/ Wilkes-Barre was not what you would consider an International one, only smaller aircraft were used and when I say small sometimes as small as a 6-12 seaters.

I remember one night I arrived from Chicago to Newark then on to Scranton. As I was waiting for the flight to be called, I heard my name being announced and as I approached the counter the pilot was there and said follow me we are going to board. As were walking, I realized that no one else was following, and when we boarded the aircraft, I noticed it was only a 6 seater; it was just me and the pilot. He asked if I would like to sit in the co-pilot's seat; I agreed, and we taxied down the runway. The sky was black, and it started to rain quite heavily with thunder and lighting. The little plane shook and vibrated in the wind and to make matters worse we were taxiing behind a 747 and someone must have flushed the toilet and caused us even more turbulence. We finally took off, and this had to be the scariest flight I have ever experienced. We were all over the sky and at times dropped a least 500 ft. When we finally landed in Scranton, I was ready to kiss the ground. I then said to the pilot I guess you are happy that the flight ends here and he replied that he was carrying mail and had to fly to Allentown next. I wished him luck and was glad that I was a sales professional not a pilot that night.

I had not yet moved my family to Scranton as I did not want to have my son change schools once again. I decided that they would move in June after school was finished. So I would commute back to Milford Mass. every other weekend. I would arrive home on Thurs. or Fri. nights and return to Scranton on Sun. night. On the way to Logan airport, I would stop at the Wharf in Boston and pick up a half a dozen 2-3 lb. live lobsters. I was still living at the Sheraton, but Juergen Persh had rented an apartment, and so it became a ritual that I would bring and cook the lobsters on Sunday nights. This of course was covered in my expense account. When I would arrive, I would open the apartment door and take the live lobsters out of the packing case and quietly place them on the floor directing them toward the living room and then wait for the fun to start. As I never knew who was there each time, the reactions were different. If some of the secretaries or female managers were there, the reaction would be a loud scream from the ladies and from the men it was different; they would comment….Norton is here. Then I would cook the lobsters and we would feast. I have a secret recipe that's to kill for and on my later trips to the Maritimes I would teach my friends and managers how to cook lobster my way.

It was 1972 and one weekend when I returned from Milford as we were landing on the mountain top at Wilkes-Barre airport, I looked out the window of the airplane and thought we were landing in a war zone. On the sides of the runways were parked dozens of military helicopters and transport planes and piled everywhere were all kinds of supplies. The first things I noticed were stacks of brooms and mops, bottled water and canned goods piled as high as the eye could see. When I debarked, I asked what was happening and I was told that while I was home hurricane Agnes had reaped havoc on the area from Allentown to Wilkes-Barre and down to Syracuse N.Y. The water rose in certain areas to 41 ft. and caused some 4.2 billion in damages and over 200 deaths. Over the years, I decided to watch as little television news as possible as it was all about disasters and doom and gloom so I did not learn of the floods until I landed. When I arrived at my hotel, there were people sleeping in the lobby and in the hallways. I was lucky that I still had my room. Luckily, Scranton is situated on higher ground and suffered minimal damage.

We were moving into the next phase with our 13 career programs ready to go to market, and we had replaced most of the field management positions; it was time to start training all the division and regional managers. I had them come in to Scranton to learn about the support from sales administration that would be available to them and to orient them about the new programs and an introduction of ICS'S teaching staff. Next step was to introduce our new sales training program which was to be used to train new and existing sales agents.

I decided to do this by one division at a time which meant dealing with only several managers at any one time. All of our new field management came from different sales organizations along with their previous training and own ideas how sales agents should be trained and I wanted to make sure they understood and accepted my sales methods and training outline. Chuck had agreed and approved my sales manual and agreed that we needed to make certain that all agents followed a unified presentation and training system throughout the country. The first day of training was always interesting as everyone had his own ideas, and I let them express them. The following 4 days were spent on understanding, learning and accepting the new methods. Each night, we would head back to the hotel for dinner and drinks, so the days were long and tiring, finishing dinner around 11 p.m. My favorite meal at the Sheraton was Prime Rib medium rare and Caesar salad with anchovies.

One night after training, several managers and I were having dinner and at a table not far from us was a beautiful young lady being wined and dined by some guy. We all noticed when she got up and went to the ladies room which was down the hall beside the coffee shop. I noticed that she was somewhat tipsy and entered the men's room by mistake. I said that I had to take a leak and asked if anyone else felt the urge. So into the john we went and standing in front of the urinal I said out loud "boy do I have to take a leak". A loud scream came from one of the stalls and out she ran. When we got back to our table, she and her friend were laughing about her experience.

After I completed the initial training of all managers, next came the follow-up training to make certain that they were following our methods of training and presentation and was this ever a challenge.

Once again, several managers at a time back to Home office for training and then back to the Sheraton for more prime rib and Caesar salads. After dinner one night, we hit the bar for a night cap, and there was a beautiful entertainer from New Jersey. After her performance, I invited her to join us for a drink. She said that she had gone sightseeing that afternoon and had walked down the hill to the shopping area. With all the managers listening, I asked her if she knew the history of Scranton. Then I told her that Scranton was built on top of all the old coal mines and that some of the coal underground was still burning. I said all those houses down the hill were in fact being heated from underground coal fires and had vents in the floor which controlled the amount of heat. Boy I must have been convincing

as the next day some of the managers asked me if it was true. We all had a good laugh.
 This was a time for me to further my skills as a National Training Director responsible for training over 650 sales agents and managers.

Lesson learned:

 If you find a mentor learn as much as you can.

Chapter 19

All progress takes place outside the comfort zone. Michael John Bobak

Now that the initial training of all managers was complete, it was time to do follow-up training with them to make certain they were using the training program effectively in teaching their agents. This was a challenge and a half as I was dealing with a strong group of individuals some who thought they had more sales and management experience then I did. Some probably did, but my experience was acquired from the school of hard knocks and that had meant learning from my own mistakes. I also had attended many motivation seminars with such pros as Zig Ziglar, W. Clement Stone, Bob Proctor, and many others over the years so I was up for the challenge.

I first checked weekly sales reports to see if there were any improvements in sales, first by Divisions, then Regions and then by agent. As I was not happy with what I saw, I decided that I should randomly drop in on training sessions being conducted by the managers without prior notice to them. What an eye opener this was; what I saw was a combination of my training mixed with other methods from other organizations or from the manager's own previous experiences. The poor agents were either totally confused and or improperly trained. One manager was training crap from the school of Scientology.

It was time to get tough, and I told the managers if they did not learn to follow the company's prescribed training they would be looking for new careers. I made it clear that it was my responsibility to make that happen as our success marketing the new career programs depended on everyone following a unified method of training and presentation. From that point, I would call the division and regional managers each week and have them recite the 10 steps in the selling process. After several weeks, things started to improve as they were now getting the idea that it was our way or the highway.

It was now time to start a recruiting blitz for new agents, and I felt we needed a recruiting procedure and training program that all managers would follow and that we could police the results. Up to this point, the managers were responsible to write and place their own recruiting ads and pay them and submit for reimbursement. I was approving about $10,000 per week in ads. I met with Gus

Becker and Chuck, and they agreed we needed a training program for recruiting and that it should be controlled by home office not left up to the field managers. I developed and wrote a recruiting manual and procedures manual and recruiting and interview forms that I felt were needed to conduct professional recruiting interviews. I then contracted with an advertising agency in New York to write a series of recruiting ads and that all ads would be placed through them. The ads were put in a binder and numbered and all the managers had to do was request the ad to be placed in the newspaper in their area and what days it was to run. I then designed a form for them to record the results of each ad placed, the number of responses, how many interviews conducted and how many were hired and scheduled for training. I then trained the division managers and issued the recruiting manuals and training to them and told them that it was their responsibility to train their regional managers in the procedures and monitor the results. The only thing I required was the weekly recruiting reports and the requests for ad placements.

After a few months of reviewing the reports, I was not satisfied with the results and I started to think my recruiting training program was not working. So I thought how do I monitor it and find the problem. ICS had a collection department calling students who were delinquent in their monthly tuition payments, but they only started calling at 10.30 a.m. so I trained some of them to call the managers who had placed ads that were currently running and try and arrange for an interview. As an example, a manager would request an ad to be placed in Saturday's paper with calls to be received from 9am -7pm.Monday and Tuesday at such and such a hotel or office.

My training program contained a script and procedure to be used on answering calls by the managers. What we discovered that the managers were seldom on location to receive calls at the time shown in the ads, sometimes only arriving 3 -4 hours later. Further, they were not using the telephone interview forms and script. A few managers were smarter than we were, and when they asked for our name, address and telephone numbers they realized that the street and telephone number we gave them did not exist in that area. So we had to get smart or get caught. Before placing calls, I would give copies of prospect leads for those cities or towns, and we would just change a street number or telephone number, and we were never caught off guard again.   I decided to record these calls and then bring in the divisional managers for retraining as it was their responsibility to use and train their managers on using the recruiting system and procedures and to monitor the results. When I played back the tapes, they did not know what to say. So, I set a new rule that if managers were first not on location at the times indicated in their ads and second that if they did not follow our recruiting procedures, than the cost of the ads would be charged back to the divisional manager and collected from their overrides. A few of the managers who were close with Chuck said that I could not do this and they would talk to Chuck. My reply was I could and would and if Chuck overrode my decision he would become the new National Training Director. Guess what: the recruiting results improved and our cost of recruiting agents was reduced as the system was now working.

Reviewing expense accounts before they were given to accounting to pay was another of my responsibilities and boy was I in for a lot of surprises. I always believed that when you work for a company you should think and act as though it was your own company and spend your allowed expense account frugally. I caught and disallowed excessive charges for laundry and booze and other non authorized expenses. I caught one manager who would take his household laundry to the hotel for washing and cleaning and charged him back the bill for $130 and boy was he angry, but he never did it again.

There is a joke about the salesman who submitted his expense account and included the cost of one Boss suit….the accounting department deducted the amount and attached a note that suits were not an approved item…..so the following week the salesman submitted his expense account and attached a note saying one Boss suit included, this time you find it!

Chuck called me into his office one day and said he had discovered that ICS had a Prison Plan for inmates and that they were only able to collect a small percentage of tuition fees and that the school was losing money on those students. He wanted to kill the program and deprive inmates the opportunity to re- educate themselves at the expense of those who did not pay their tuition. I said I would put on my thinking cap and see what I could come up with to solve the problem.

I went back to my office and did some research and found that a high percentage of inmates were former military, and I knew that they had military education benefits as veterans worth several thousand dollars. Next, I discovered that when you are in prison the Warden has Power of Attorney and acts on your behalf.

 Military benefits are paid by the government upon a form submited by the school and students certifying that the lessons were complete. Now is when my creative juices started to flow. How could I make certain we were paid our tuition fees on time with no exceptions? I made up a new enrollment agreement that had to be signed by the student and warden as Power of Attorney. The warden would have to then sign the required form that lessons were in fact completed, and we listed ICS's address for payment of tuition fees from the department of Veterans affairs. I then went to see our attorney to check the proper wording. I then presented my solution to Chuck and he said it was great…but then he said what about the non veterans how do we collect from them. Back to my office I went and put on my thinking cap.

Two days later, I solved the problem; it was so simple that it was stupid for someone not to think about it before. Simply, if a non veteran wanted to enroll, he must have someone outside of the prison agree to pay his tuition and must sign an agreement to that fact. Second problem solved and we had no more collection problems and the prison plan now became very profitable as we had a " captured" audience who wanted to learn and many enrolled in more than one program as they had a lot of "time" on their hands.

Lessons learned:

I was becoming smarter with each new challenge using my creativity abilities and plain simple common sense to solve problems and workable solutions.

Chapter 20

Your attitude not your aptitude will determine your altitude. Zig Ziglar

There was never a dull moment working as the National Training Director at ICS. I had a great opportunity to use and develop my creative abilities and some that even I did not know I possessed.

We required and used one enrollment application which covered every state regulation and was governed by federal rules. But as the various states become more autonomous, each state applied different rules specifically to cooling off period rules. It started with one state requiring us to print a new application and soon became 50. What a joke; talk about bureaucratic power hungry idiots. Federal requirements were adequate to cover all states but not good enough for the power hungry civil servants.

So, Chuck gave the job to rewrite and print new applications to a staff executive who had some legal background and experience. He did not understand the importance to fulfill each state requirement within the time allowed. Chuck blew his cork when we were delinquent and were ordered to stop selling in that state until we had the proper application. So guess who ended-up becoming a half ass lawyer and enrollment application designer responsible for writing and printing the required applications......me!

I wrote all the legal changes but reviewed them with our lawyer to make certain we met the new requirements before printing. I never knew I had legal smarts to write in the proper legal jargon.

Corporate then stuck us with a new V.P. of marketing which Chuck was not happy about as he came from the book publishing business and knew nothing about the school business. Gus Becker who was then the V.P. sales was not happy either as he had expressed to Chuck that he wanted that position. The plan was he would move to V.P. of marketing, and I would move to V.P. of sales. He had told Chuck that if he did not get the position he would leave and ultimately he did. I respected him as a man of his words but hated losing him as an associate, my mentor and friend. He was the only mentor that I learned anything from, my other learning came from was the school of hard knocks.

Next, I was asked to spend time with the new V.P. marketing and give him a general overview of our marketing and programs and then arrange for him to go on sales calls with one of our regional sales managers. I arranged for him to spend a few days with our manager in the Baltimore area. They went out on their first call at 10a.m. and then returned to the hotel for lunch as their next call was at 3.p.m. At lunch, we found out he was an alcoholic and had a few too many and when they were ready to go on the next call here's what happened which gave him an insight to what some agents had to contend with in the real world of selling. The regional manager and the new V.P. walked out to the parking lot and got in the car, started the engine and put the car in gear and nothing happened; they did not move forward one inch. They got out of the car to inspect the reason and discovered the car was up on blocks and all 4 wheels were missing. Chuck asked me how I arranged that and I replied "me no tell".

Not only did we acquire the new V.P of marketing who did not last very long in the position but we also acquired a new Chairman of the board who also came from the book publishing side of the business. I guess that I did a good job in working with the first one or helping get rid of him that Chuck asked me to do an introduction and explanation of our marketing materials for the new Chairman.

I first prepared copies of our advertising materials and next copies of our fulfillment brochures for each program; then, I went into the mail room and collected an assortment of leads that had been mailed in by prospects. We used matchbooks advertising very successfully. Some of the return coupons that had postage paid stamps came in envelopes with regular postage stamps applied. I noticed an unusual request for information pinned on a bulletin board with the envelope it came in, and I read it and laughed. It was from somewhere in Arkansas and it read "please send me inffermaton on the T.V.progim"; funnier still, it was printed on a piece of toilet paper. I took it and went to our creative department and asked them to frame it for my presentation.

A few days later, I was ready to do my presentation. We met in the corporate meeting room. Attending were the new Chairman, Chuck and me. I started explaining our new career programs, our advertising and fulfillment brochures and then the various reply cards.. I explained that even though many of our reply cards were postage paid we still received many in envelopes with postage stamps. Up to this point, I was getting the thumbs-up signal from Chuck.

I then took the request on toilet paper which was now framed and backed on a wine colored piece of material under glass and explained that we get some unusual requests. I handed the frame to the Chairman who when he first looked had a weird expression on his face. Chuck gave me a dirty angry look .When the Chairman realized that the request was printed on toilet paper, he then broke into laughter. He asked if he could keep it, and I agreed and would you believe he hung it in his office. We became close over the next few months as he respected my position and my results.

ICS had an office in Montreal that was responsible for Canadian sales and that reported directly to corporate, not to Chuck in the USA. It had their own President and V.P of sales and regional managers. They were still marketing and selling ICS's old programs and were like the USA division before them running in the red. So another call into Chuck's office and the request this time was to go see the Chairman who had requested that I fly up to Montreal and show them what we were now doing in the USA. When I saw the Chairman he said take your family, spend a few days at the Montreal office and then take a few days off to ski before returning, all at the company's expense. So off I went having no idea how I would be received.

When I arrive for my first meeting, it was a repeat of my first few weeks at ICS. They considered it their turf and that they were operating in the same manner as the previous divisional directors in the USA. I was considered the enemy and, I guess, the Jew boy from head office. Whatever I explained to them the first morning, they showed no interest and stated they were happy in the way they were operating. They did not know that I was aware they were operating in the red and that's why the Chairman asked me to explain our success in the USA with our new career programs. After a negative receptive morning, we all went to lunch, and I was surprised we went to a pub and everyone ordered a few beers and then we had steaks. We were all given separate bills, and the Canadian president did not even have the decency to pick up my tab.

So back to the office we went, and I started the afternoon session by stating that I was sent here by the Chairman of the board to explain what we had achieved in the USA and I personally did not give a damn what they did or did not do here in the Canadian operation, so please have the decency to listen. The afternoon session was somewhat better, and after, I felt it was time for me to head up to Ste.Sauveur and ski for a couple of days.

Riding up on the chair lift, I had time to reflect on my meeting and decided that I did not learn anything about the Canadian operation and its procedures, so I decided to head back and spend a few days of investigation. The President was not happy at my return but allowed me free reign to visit with each department and staff. I then headed back to Scranton to give my report to the Chairman which wasn't pretty. A few days later, Chuck called me into his office and said the chairman wanted me to go back to Montreal and work with the V.P. of sales and teach him how to recruit and train using my methods.

What a waste of time this turned out to be. You can only teach the teachable and those willing to learn, not those who think they know it all. I made several trips teaching him our recruiting methods and conducting training sessions for new agents. On what turned out to be my last trip, we had hired 7 new agents and I decided that it was time for the V.P. to get his feet wet and conduct the training on his own. So back to Scranton I went.

Training was to start on Monday and completed by Friday. On Tuesday, I decided to call and check on how things were going and could not reach the V.P. in the training room or in his room at the motel. After several attempts, I finally reached one of the new agents on Wednesday morning. He said that they started training on Monday, but when they had gone to the training room on Tuesday morning, there was a sign saying that the V. P. was called to Scranton and they should study on their own. I was in Scranton and no sign of the V.P., so I booked a flight and headed back to Toronto. Four of the new hires had packed up and returned home, disappointed in how poorly the first day of training was. I managed to save three and spent the rest of the week training them. I called the V.P.'s home several times and finally his wife answered and I asked where he was; she said he was in retreat, whatever that meant, and would see me on Monday morning.

Monday morning I decided to pay the bill for the rooms and meals so I could head back to Scranton after meeting the V.P. I noticed a bar bill on his room charge for $170 and now I understood what retreat meant. At 10 am, the V.P. showed up and I was pretty pissed off having wasted my time over the last 3 months and told him so. I, in my anger, told him that he no longer worked for the company and that his bar bill would be deducted from his termination pay. He said you can't fire me I'm a V.P. a position higher than you. I said I just did, and he said he would talk to Lew Robinson the V.P of sales in Scranton I answered that you can talk to the man in the moon if you wish but my decision was final and if I was overridden by any higher-ups they could have my job.

Back to Scranton and a meeting with Chuck. He asked how things went with the training of the new hires, and I told him what happened. I then said you no longer have a V.P. of sales in Canada as I had fired him. Chuck said you don't have that authority and I placed the room charge in front of him and said if you want to keep him then you go train him yourself.

 I reported the same to the Chairman and that afternoon I was told to head back to Montreal and take over the sales management position.

From National training Director to Canadian Sales Manager and back in my hometown Montreal.

Lessons learned:

There are times in life when you need to take the imitative and go beyond your scope of authority to do the right things that are best for the company you work for

Chapter 21

Expect problems and eat them for breakfast. Alfred A. Montaport

Moving back to Montreal to take over as the sales manager brought on many new challenges, but with all that I had learned working in the USA and England it was an easy adjustment.

In the first few weeks, all previous sales management staff were terminated from the president on down. It was me alone, and first I had to win the confidence of the administrative staff of which some had been with the company for more than 20-30 years. Again, I was first considered a threat; also, being the only Jew did not help. I had gone thru all that crap in the USA and was able to win over most in a few short weeks.

Chuck Miller decided that the Canadian operation needed an administration President and decided it was time to find a new home for Juergen Persh who was his Joe- boy in the USA and would be his eyes and ears in Canada. I guess he still had not learned that Juergen was what we called in the corporate world the JACKAL. A Jackal is only interested in his own success even at the expense of others. A jackal would try and kill-off any competition to gain his own power and success at whatever cost.

Well, here I once again had to deal with Juergen the Jackal. Let me explain a theory that I had developed about certain types of individuals in the corporate world. I noticed that short in stature individuals suffered from some personality traits and in dealing with others were authoritative and power hungry.

This was a true picture of Juergen. The minute he landed in Montreal, he showed once again his true colors and personality. His forte was motivation by fear.

I saw the same traits in Lee Curtis who was my Regional Director when I first moved to the USA with Famous Artists Schools and again with Juergen in England.

Power in the wrong hands creates all kinds of problems for those working with them, and, in many cases, it also bites them in the ass as well.

Juergen not only tried to control all the people in the administrative department but me and my staff as well. The fun started once again.

In the corporate jungle there are different players trying to climb the corporate ladder and I give them some titles.

1. The builder who works as though he owns the company.
2. The politician who play politics to keep his job.
3. The maintainer who is satisfied with where he is and just does his 9-5 job.
4. The jackal that pretends to be everybody's friend but is only interested in killing off any competition that gets in his way in climbing to the next level.
5. And then there is the incompetent who has reached his or her level of incompetence.

Back to Juergen, I had to make it clear that I would not accept any interference in the daily operation of my area of responsibility, and that without sales we would not need him or any administrative staff.

He was jealous of my ongoing increases in my income and tried several times to reduce it, but each time I would come up with some new marketing ideas that increased my income. Boy was he pissed when he had to sign my override cheques.

I presented my first year sales goals to Chuck and went to work. Screw the politics. My goal was to hire and train 25 new agents in Ontario and the Maritime provinces by the end of the year, and I achieved that goal without a hitch in 6 months.

Agents that I had worked with and managed with Famous Artists Schools a joined my team as soon as they heard I was back in Canada. These were top producers, so I not only met my hiring goals quickly but surpassed my sales goals as well.

Chuck was more than excited with the results, and I was to receive a promotion to the next level and increase in pay and overrides.

I organized a sales meeting in Toronto with my managers and top agents to celebrate our achievements, and Juergen joined us. He was to announce my promotion to V.P. of Canadian sales, but being the Jackal that he was and jealous of my promotion, he decided to announce the appointment as Assistant V.P. what a joke.

My managers were shocked and decided to go and buy me a gift, a beautiful pen and pencil set with an onyx base and they took it upon themselves to have it engraved. They presented it to me at dinner that evening. When they handed it to me, it was engraved with my name and the title read VICE PRESIDENT OF SALES. They passed it around the table, and when Juergen read the inscription, he did a double take. The idiot had the nerve and stupidity to announce asst. V.P.

when there was no V.P. for me to be an assistant to. The Jackal made a jackass of himself and really showed his colors and lost all credibility with my sales force.

Lesson learned:

In the corporate world you're never done with office politics.

Chapter 22

Don't take life to seriously, you will never get out alive.   Elbert Hubbard

Juergen's style of management, motivation by fear and to control everyone and everything for most would have been a stressful way of working with him. I just took it in my stride, and as I planned my own travel schedules, managing all of Canada kept me out of the office and him out of my hair for 3 weeks a month.
As the sales force increased in numbers and our sales quotas were met with ease, my job became more of being a social director and motivator. I planned incentive trips for my top producers each year to go to some exotic islands. My *management* skills required me to wear many different hats. I became a family counselor, a financial advisor, a marriage counselor, and, more importantly, a friend, and we became one big happy family.
As my income from not only my base salary but my over-ride commissions on sales increased, Juergen attempted to reduce my commissions as he became even more jealous that my earnings were more than his. He tried to reduce my advertising budget which would have reduced my earnings. So, I proposed a new bonus structure for personally developed business. My agents and I would receive higher commissions as it reduced the company's costs of producing sales. I developed a referral program for clients who received a gift for referrals who enrolled in one of our programs. The result was more sales and more income for me. Juergen was not a happy camper as my income again surpassed his.
There's always a way to skin a cat; all you need is a little creativity.
The next four years went by rapidly, and life was good as far as my career, but on the home front things got gradually worse. As I grew in my career, my wife's life went in the opposite direction. It was like we had nothing in common. I liked to ski, take my son fishing, and teach him how to play tennis, while she vegetated. She did not want to go on trips or be part of any company activities. She did not like herself as she was either too fat or too thin and had no real interests in life. My travelling did not help our situation, and I knew the end was coming as we were now living like we were sharing a house, not a home.
When I look back, our marriage would have ended a lot sooner if I did not travel as much as I did.

My wife's sister was somewhat of an expert on divorce and how to bleed a man for everything she could get as she had just gone through her second divorce and recommended her lawyer to my wife. So one Monday morning, my secretary came into my office and told me a gentleman was here to see me. I told her to send him in and when he entered my office he said he was a bailiff and handed me separation documents. Even though I was expecting this to happen at one point, reality was still a shock. I put on my jacket and told my secretary that I would call her later that afternoon; she sensed something was wrong and I told her I would talk to her later.

I got into my car, and I drove to St. Sauveur as the day before I had been looking at the ski cottages for rent in the Montreal Gazette. There was an ad that stood out; it read "country home for rent for ski season" and somehow I remembered the address 22 Aubry St. St.Sauveur. I drove around and ended up right in front of the house. I decided to at least take a look as I would soon need a place to live. The owner was a retired insurance executive and his wife, and they were looking for someone responsible to look after their home for the winter months as they wanted to go to Florida. The house was fully furnished with a view facing the ski hill, and at night you could see the hill all lit up.

I asked how much he wanted in rent for the next 5 months, and he asked if $2,000 was too much. I took out my cheque book and gave him a cheque for the total and asked when he would be ready to leave for Florida. He answered they would leave by 5p.m. the next night.

I then got back in my car and called my lawyer and drove back to Montreal to his office to look at the separation document that I was handed that morning. The documents were prepared by a Jewish Lawyer for a Jewish princess and assumed that I was a millionaire. We laughed, and as we reviewed the terms, I became very angry. Her lawyer wanted not only my blood but to keep her in a lifestyle that only the very rich could afford. I stated that after being served I could no longer stay at home, and he advised me that if I moved out before we came to an agreement it would not be a good idea. He said you travel a lot; go home and pack a bag and tell her you are going on a sales trip out west. I packed a bag, and the next morning I went to the office and at 5p.m. drove to St.Sauveur and spent the week getting used to being single again. I could have stayed in Montreal and rented an apartment but the idea of now being able to be a part time ski bum appealed to me even though I have to drive one hour to and from the office each day.

What I needed was fresh air and time to start living after many unhappy years in a bad marriage.

At the end of the week after meeting with my lawyer, I met with my soon to be separated wife and told her what I was prepared to do to support her and my son and that she should go back to school to learn a career so she could build a life for herself. She said that she was not prepared to accept less than what her lawyer had asked for in the separation agreement. I assume her sister the expert was counseling her, and I said if she thought she could take me to the cleaners, that she should think wisely as I was prepared to quit my job and become a full time ski bum, and she would get nothing, and if she thought that I was kidding, she should think again as I loved skiing and would welcome the break from the everyday rat race.

We settled, and I permanently moved out. I became a weekend and night time ski bum. It was the best winter I ever had. It was like being born again. Living in St. Sauveur in a quaint little village brought me back to nature and I guess that in the not too distant future I would eventually live in the country as city life was not something I enjoyed.

I was then 42 years old and earning a good income with a good transportable career as a professional sale executive.

 As soon as the word got out that I was separated, things started to happen, and at a Christmas party a few weeks later, I met a friend of one of our office staff who was 21 years old and separated. Her name was Carole and she was gorgeous. I found out that she loved to ski. You figure the rest. Yep! You are right; she became my ski partner for that winter, and we had a relationship for a few years after that. So from an unhappy, unfulfilling marriage to being born again at 42, life was good. My friends saw me on the hills skiing with Carole they must have thought what a lucky bastard and were jealous as hell. My separated wife got reports from some of her family that also skied on the same hills and I'm sure she had a bird.

Being free again and traveling all over Canada each week meeting with my managers and agents and then spending the weekends with my son or ski partner was great. My agents and managers were all well trained to my sales procedures so my life took on a new role back to being a social director like I was in high school.

Lessons learned:

Life is too short and to be unhappy and sometimes you have to make some serious decisions, which is not easy to do especially when a child is involved.

Chapter 23

When I look back at my first marriage and some of the reasons it did not work, I think the biggest was that we really never became friends, and as I learned later in life, friendship was the most important element in making a relationship work. Next was trust, and as you remember my early childhood experience with my father, without trust there could never be a close relationship. Finally, honesty plays an important role as well. None of these elements existed in our marriage, so it was doomed to fail.
Here I was once again building my wall of protection so I would not be hurt by another relationship.

 Lessons learned:

What had I learned from these negative experiences? Keep your feelings to yourself and do not let anyone come too close, and you will never get hurt. Boy was I wrong because you will never experience true love. Here I was at 42 years of age with half of my life gone by and never having experienced love in the true sense. My experiences of love was for my son, and over the years, my horses and dogs but with half my life having gone south, love for a women did not exist for me.

Chapter 24

It was now 1977, and I had been busy building my sales team from coast to coast and that meant that I was busy traveling, recruiting and training new agents in every province. My sales team was stable with very little turnover, and it was time to appoint some sales managers to look after the agents on a daily basis.
I appointed a manager in B.C. and in Calgary,
 Toronto and the Maritimes, and my role changed from sales manager to more like the godfather. In my new role, I wore many hats which helped motivate my team to top sales results. I became more of a friend then a boss to my managers and agents and their families.
At times, I was a father confessor, a marriage counselor, a financial advisor and sometimes a bankruptcy advisor but most of all not just the boss but a friend who was concerned about their well being.
I used all of my skills to keep the team motivated, and that took on new challenges. If what motivated one agent was a fishing trip or a day of golf or skiing or boating or winning a sales contest or qualifying for a one or two week trip to an exotic island. The result was a highly motivated team of top producers and for me an opportunity to hone my skills at the things I enjoyed most.
When agents achieved their monthly sales goals, I would reward them by taking them and their wives or significant others out to dinner at one of the finest restaurants in the area which was something I learned from the only mentor I had the pleasure of spending time with. His name was Gus Becker whom I worked with in the U.S. He knew every fine food establishment in every state, and his reward for this knowledge was a bad case of the gout.
Developing trust and earning respect and loyalty from agents took time and considerable effort in most cases as their previous relationship with their supervisors or bosses left a lot to be desired. Many managers motivated their agents by fear and did not understand what it took to motivate and properly train a sales team of professionals.
Motivation is not easy to do on your own in many cases you need to associate with self motivated people. The opposite of motivation in my view is procrastination and many people suffer from this disease. Motivation comes from positive thinking and in today's world with all the negative things happening in our lives is

sometimes difficult to come by. Negative thoughts on the other hand tend to breed like rabbits and are not easy to get rid of.

On a trip to Winnipeg in 1979 working with one of my agents, we were talking about dreams and goals, and he told me that his dream was that he wanted to learn how to fly an airplane. Some of us have dreams at some point of being able to fly. I told him I always wanted to learn to fly as well, but in an airplane not just jumping off some mountain and taking flight. I told him that I almost took lessons when I was working in Minnesota as I was flying all over that state and Wisconsin and that possibly owning an airplane made some sense at the time in managing the territory.

On my next trip, I landed in Winnipeg on a Friday to conduct a training session and planned to stay the weekend. The Agent whose name was Al Hunkin told me he was in communication with a pilot in Minnesota who had designed an Ultralight airplane, and we decided to drive down and take a look.

What we saw was a hang glider with a motor and a swing seat but no landing gear, and we asked how it worked. So, out of his garage and onto his back lawn we went. He bent down on one knee holding the frame of this so called Ultralight, pushed the starter button and the motor which was mounted behind him came to life, spinning the propeller. He then stood up and started to run taking maybe 10 steps and was airborne. We were in awe of this Dacron colored, so- called airplane with a wingspan that was 32ft. across. He maneuvered left and right by swinging his body in the direction he wanted to turn. To go up or down, he moved forward or backward.

 We watched him for about 30 minutes and then started to wonder how he would land without a landing gear or wheels. As they say, what goes up must come down, and he turned into the wind and prepared to land. This was a sight to see because as he approached the ground, his feet started a running motion, and when he was a few feet from the ground, he shut off the engine and landed on his feet in less than 15 feet from where he touched down. The whole airplane with motor weighed less than 125 pounds so he gently placed it on the ground.

He asked if we would like to give it a try and after giving us some basic flight instruction, we felt we were ready. Up! Up! And away into the wild blue yonder we went. Al went first and landed without incident. I went second, and when I landed, I almost took down the fence in his backyard, but we survived. We decided to stay the night and give it a second try the next morning. When we arrived, the wind was up, and we let him do another demonstration. The stall speed was 22 mph, and the wind was probably 25mph so once he was airborne, he throttled back to 22 mph and it looked from the ground that he was not moving. Over dinner the night before, Al and I had discussed if we could possibly manufacture and sell these Ultralights in Canada. I felt that with modifications and installing a landing gear and teaching would- be pilots like ourselves how to fly, that there was definitely a market. So you guessed it; I bought the prototype. This was the start of a whole new venture and challenge for me to use my marketing skills.

Al was responsible to run the business and I, still working at ICS, developed a marketing plan in my spare time of which I had lots of as my sales team was stable and producing excellent sales results. It was the challenge I needed at the time.

I felt that the new sport of learning to fly and owning an Ultralight (excuse the pun) would take off and be a new challenging business opportunity.

The challenge of learning something I knew nothing about would once again stimulate my creativity and be fun and profitable. That's what entrepreneurship is all about.

Lesson learned:

Every man at one time or another dreams of taking flight, and I was no different. For me it was a new challenge to use my creative abilities in an area I knew nothing about.

Don't be afraid of new to venture into new opportunities.

Chapter 25

Back to recruiting and training, I hired a new agent in Ottawa who had just emigrated from the USA with his wife who had family in Ottawa. We became instant friends as we discovered that we had a lot in common. His name was John Gillen, and he quickly became a top producer. In his 3rd month, he exceeded his sales quota by 50%, and I took him and his wife out to dinner as a reward. Over dinner and the rest of the evening as we got to know more about each other, I had a feeling that we were all bound to become lifetime friends.

Her maiden name was Ingrid von Luczenbacher, and she originally was from Hungary. In later years I found out what the "von" in her name meant it was a nobility title. Her father was in fact a Count in Hungary and as such she was a countess and as I got to know her more she sure was a countess in many ways.

She met John while working for the same company in the USA, and John, recently divorced, fell madly in love with this beautiful lady. John unlike me was a romantic and knew how to charm Ingrid and win her as his bride.

As time went by, I learned more about their lives and they learned about mine. John had five children from his first marriage, and Ingrid became a second mother to them on weekend and summer visits. They wanted their own children, but Ingrid could not conceive, and they decided to adopt. I also found out some of the reasons for his divorce from his first wife. John was an alcoholic, and this was partly to blame for the divorce. Ingrid, like most wives, thought she could cure his drinking, not realizing that alcoholism is a disease and very difficult to cure. I think that adopting children was a way to keep their marriage together. Their first adoption was a boy of 4 who they named Dan who had been in several foster homes and needed lots of love and attention. The second was a 6 month old girl who they named Erin. I became their adopted uncle. I remember the first time I visited and saw this beautiful blond little girl, and when I tried to hold her, she cried. She had become so attached to Ingrid that only she could hold her. They all became my second family.

This was probably the first time I experienced a true friend who was a woman.

Chapter 26

Believe you can and you're half way there.

The next few years passed quickly except for my ongoing problems of having to work with a bureaucratic idiot who only knew how to manage by fear and not by motivation. I was lucky that I controlled my travel, so I spent most of my time in the field with my managers and agents.

On a trip to Manitoba one of my agents had arranged a motivation seminar in Brandon with the guest speaker being Zig Ziglar. He flew into Winnipeg and we arranged for a private Cessna to fly us to Brandon. Here I was sitting next to Zig that I had met before at one of the Success seminars. When we arrived at the motel where the seminar was to take place Zig went up to the reception desk and asked the young lady if she had any rooms available. She replied that they were all booked and Zig said, if the Prime Minister of Canada were to come here tonight , would you find him a room. Flustered she said I guess I would and Zig said I have it on good authority that he is not coming, so I will take his room.

He then said who he was and that he wanted to check –in. She asked him for a credit card and he opened his wallet and gave her a card marked credit card. She tried to process it and of course it was a fake.

He said you asked me for a credit card and I gave you one. We all laughed. The next day was a lot of fun and learning about motivation. At one point Zig said when I ask people to do things they say I will do it when I get around to it. At that point he started tossing out round cardboard disks with the word printed TOUIT!, and he said now you have a round "TOUIT" go do it. I still have a picture of us together and a personally signed book he wrote, "See You At The Top".

 Back to reality, Jurgen was busy playing politics with Chuck Miller President of ICS and protecting his ass being the jackal he was. My sales results made him look good and I'm sure he thought it was all his doing. The administrative staff all hated his guts and my agents had no respect for him as well. This was my continuing education about the Corporate Jungle and the Peter Principle.

In the early 1999 American Schools out of California indicated an interest in purchasing ICS and immediately Jurgen started playing politics with the owners to protect his ass. He sold out Chuck Miller who had hired him when he was down and out and promoted him to his current position. He had no loyalty, only greed for himself.

He went to California to meet the potential owners and when he returned I met with him over a long lunch and asked him why they were interested in the purchase as they operated a strictly mail sales operation. I asked him if their intent was to turn ICS in a mail sales operation and he said absolutely not. At that time over 90% of sales came from my agents and only a few sales in areas where we had no agents came in by mail. The way he said it and his body language told me otherwise.

 They purchased ICS and Chuck Miller was out of a job, but Jurgen was safe as he had played his cards right. Within a month he started stealing leads from my marketing budget and started trying to sell our programs by mail. I saw the handwriting on the wall and decided to wait until the first quarterly review before making any decisions.

When Jurgen returned from California after the review we again met over a 3 hour lunch and during our conversation I again asked what the intent of the new owners was, and once again his body language confirmed that he had lied to me. It was in fact the new owner's intent over that they would market our programs 100% by mail. What he did not know was that I had flown to California had met with the new owners and I sensed that this was their intent.

We were having an after dinner drink and I toasted the future success of the company and told him that I was tendering my resignation effective immediately. The shocked look on his face was worth all the crap I had to deal with him over the years.

He asked why I and I told him that he made the mistake of lying to me not once but twice and in my court two strikes meant out. I told him that I was a builder not a destroyer and if he wanted to destroy the sales force that he would have to do it himself.

In 1979 my earning were over $75,000 a year with all expenses paid was not a bad income, but my integrity was worth more than that. Besides I needed some R and R and a change.

Over that weekend I took stock of myself and thought about some of the things I had wanted to do over the last several years and I made a list. One was to take a sailing course and on Sunday I noticed an ad in the Montreal Gazette for a course starting on Monday in Lake St. Louis in Pointe Claire and guess what…Monday I was sailing or should I say being flipped overboard several times a day, at least for the first few days. I was having a great time, clearing my mind from the everyday grind.

Lessons learned:

When you no longer trust the people you work with or the company it's time to move on.

Chapter 27

Don't dwell on the past just chock it up as another learning experience.

I was into my 6th day of semi- retirement waterlogged and starting to unwind when on Thursday night at about 10.30, I received a call from one of my agents who had terminated his employment with ICS when he heard I had resigned. He had just been interviewed by a company in Toronto.
During his interview, the CEO told him that they had been looking for an experienced sales manager, and he dropped my name. When he called, he asked if it was o.k. for the CEO to call me that night. I said I was not prepared to go back to work, but I agreed to at least talk to the CEO.
Thirty minutes later at 11 pm, the phone rang, and a gentleman with a booming voice said that he was in Winnipeg, but he was flying to Montreal the next morning specifically to meet with me over dinner and drinks at the Four Seasons Hotel. He wanted to meet at 4p.m so I agreed because it still gave me time to take a sailing lesson that morning. Who was I to refuse a good meal, so I agreed. Besides, I was curious to find out more about this company and why this sudden interest in me.
His name was George McQuat, and the company was Canadian American Financial Corporation, a division of North American Life and Casualty out of Minneapolis in the USA. The company was at the time the marketing arm for Canadian Scholarship Trust Plan selling education savings programs. Weird or what! I had sold education savings programs when I was managing a seniors' home and selling for Famous Schools in the mid 60's, 20 years earlier.
At that time, it was a cooperative savings plan when members pooled their funds to earn higher interest. Now it was an RESP (Registered Education Savings Plan). Here I was just starting to enjoy my new found freedom with plans to finally become a ski bum for the winter and now less than one week after my period of retreat was being interviewed for a new executive position.
It was one of the longest interviews that I have had lasting from 4pm. to almost midnight. My first impression of George McQuat was that he looked more like a chairman of the board than a CEO, complete with a puff in his jacket pocket and flowers pinned to his lapel. This as I found out later, was his mark.

George had worked his way up to management in the insurance industry and as I got to know him better was still stuck in that time warp. I will tell you more about him later.

During dinner as far as George was concerned, he had found the man he was looking for and offered me the position of director of agencies, a title he had brought down from the insurance industry. I told him that I was not ready to start a new career at this time, but he persisted and invited me to visit their offices in the Money Life Building in Toronto the following Friday. A few after dinner drinks later, I agreed to visit.

After visiting his office, he said he would prepare an offer of employment and courier it to me the following week. So back I went to continue my sailing course. His offer arrived a few days later and it was for less income than I had been earning at ICS so I told that I was not interested. When he asked why I said why would I move to Toronto and earn less than I had previously earned! He thought he had lost me and a few days later told me to propose my own compensation plan.

 I proposed my own compensation plan which consisted of a reasonable salary but increased overrides on increased sales.and he accepted it without question. So much for being a ski bum that winter instead I was now a Director of Agencies whatever that meant. Just a new executive title to add to my resume. Funny part is I never had to prepare one as my reputation in the direct sales arena was well known and I never in my many careers had to use one.

 I believed that when an opportunity presents itself and you see potential take the leap if it works out great and if not chalk it up as another learning experience and move on to your next opportunity.

The office staff consisted of an office manager whose name was Doreen Johnston and a assistant Janice Brady who did some of the bookkeeping without any financial education. A student came in to help with filing after school and her name was Nancy Oulton who was later to become full time. Not much of a marketing team with little or no knowledge on what it took to build and motivate a sales organization.

Lessons learned:

I was never afraid of failure as I considered it another of life's learning experiences Just learn to never repeat them. Life should not be about collecting failures but using those failures as a stepping stone to success.

You must always be open to new ideas and opportunities.

I

Chapter 28

Listen first talk later.

Part of my compensation was that CAFC was to pay for my accommodations in Toronto and flights back to Montreal every other week as my son had started school, and I did not want to move him until I was sure that the position was what I really wanted and that he finish school that year.

My accommodation was at the Inn on the Park a block away from the office, and my room was booked on a monthly basis so I would not have to remove my personal belongings while traveling.

Now, I had to evaluate the staff I would be working with and that was not too difficult a task as the total staff consisted of three. The sales management consisted of the boss, George McQuat and another Director of Agencies whose name was John Atkins and now me the new boy on the block.

The field sales force consisted of what was called Enrollment directors who ran their own agencies with little or almost nonexistent support from home office.

So, let's look at each of my new partners in crime individually, an interesting group for sure and how they reacted to me being hired.

George suggested that I invite the office manager whose name was Doreen for lunch or dinner so we could get to know each other. So, I went into her office and she did not even acknowledge my presence. When she finally looked up she asked abruptly what I wanted, and I said that George had suggested that we have lunch and get to know each other. She responded that she was too busy so I decided screw her and her attitude. I would get to know her on my time or not at all.

Next, was the bookkeeper; her name was Janice, a young lady of about 19 who had no schooling in accounting but was doing the best she could. In later years, she finally enrolled in some accounting courses. She was more friendly but reserved.

The next one was a file clerk, Nancy, who worked part time but in later years became a member of the full time staff; she was probably the friendliest of all.

Then there was John Atkins who was the other director of agencies. John as I soon discovered, was an alcoholic in training and later to become a full fledged raving alcoholic. I guess George was desperate when he hired him. His people skills and sales management skills were close to zero. To give you an example, when a new agent in training asked him how to get leads of families with young children, the idiot threw the telephone book at him.

Then there was George the head honcho; he was a study all to himself. He had to be in total control of every aspect of the business and found it difficult to pass on responsibilities. He was what Italians considered the El Capo.

His rise to the top was in the insurance industry, and his training and management style was insurance related.

In my first management meeting with him, I asked what my duties and responsibilities were and what he expected of me in the short term.

His answer was he did not expect me to contribute much in the first year; all I had to do was travel across the country and meet with the Enrollment Directors, to take them and their significant others to dinner and not much more. I could see myself becoming a vegetable and possibly a raving alcoholic as well. A good start to my new career.

I asked what type of accommodations I should use when travelling and was told five stars as we had to show success as a company.

Well, off I went to meet the Enrolment Directors, an eye opening experience.

I started in B.C. with the two existing Enrolment directors whose names were John Papp and Richard Gleig. I invited them for lunch at the Four Seasons Hotel, and when we sat down, even before looking at the menu, their first words were,(who the f---k are you? another home office idiot!) What a great welcome for their new Director of Agencies; it was probably the best of the worst that I had experienced in all my dealings with agents and managers over the years.

At this point, I wondered if I should have opted to become a ski bum instead of accepting George's offer.

But I saw this reaction as a challenge and an opportunity to win them over, not a difficult task as I had been through this same shit several times before with Famous Schools and ICS.

 The field sales force vs home office administration exists in every company. The sales agents think that home office staffs are idiots as they do not understand what the sales agents have to do to write business and the office staff thinks the sales agents are a bunch of thieves and that they are earning too much. So much for stupidity on both sides.

I told them that I agreed that in a lot of companies there are idiots both in home office and in the field sales organizations and that I had experienced them as well, but for their information, I was not one of them.

I explained that even though the company paid me I worked for the betterment of the sales force and that I would side and support whatever side was right. I could see that they were skeptical and that I would have to win their trust. I then asked how I could help them, and for the next hour, I listened to all their frustrations with home office and the lack of support and marketing materials. So much for my first meeting with the sales force.

For the next month, I travelled from one end of the country to the other, and it was the same reaction to the lack of support from home office and that they were in bad need of some support from management, training and marketing materials.

I asked about the support from John Atkins who was their director of agencies, and they confirmed my evaluation that he was an idiot and a drunk.

Back to home office I went and decided not to tell George how the Enrolment director's felt. He asked what my next plans were, and I said I would be behind closed doors in my office for the next 30 to 60 days to develop some new marketing materials. His reaction was he felt that we had sufficient materials but allowed me to suggest and develop new ones for his approval.

This new position was going to take a lot of my learned skills.

Lessons learned:

Remember as you move through life you are learning for a reason even though you at the time might not know what that reason is.

Chapter 29

Now, I was in my realm putting all my creative abilities to work.

George told me that in a few months the CST foundation would be celebrating their 20th anniversary, and it would be a grand black tie dinner with all the members of the Foundation board and all the Enrollment directors present.

So, I set my target to have all of my new marketing materials ready for presentation by then. I also decided not to tell or show George or anyone else what I was working on as he had made a comment that all the sales force needed was possibly a new brochure as the one currently being used was over 20 years old and had never been updated. The baby on the brochure was probably old enough to retire.

What I also learned that there was bad blood between George and the CST Foundation as both sides were control freaks. The Foundation was non- profit and we the marketing company under contract was highly profitable. Here, it was administration against sales administration.

What I learned was that the Foundation board had the exclusive rights to approve all marketing and promotional materials to be used. This was part of the problem. So, not only did I have to develop new materials but needed to win over the board members. I decided to make friends with the Foundation staff as the new guy on the block with no past history. I became one of the only members of our group that was welcome in their offices which were two floors down.

Over the years, I learned that for marketing to work you need to not only develop pre-sale materials but also after- sale tools as well. So I made my list and checked it twice and over the next couple of months designed 10 new tools, one that we had used successfully at ICS which was a dispenser for the new brochures.

It was tough to keep all this under wraps, so I introduced some sales reports which I presented to George which he turned down as he felt the Enrollment directors did not need them.

I had all my new materials ready in mechanical form and ready to print as I was told that I needed the Foundation's approval before printing. The board meeting was scheduled for one day before the big 20th anniversary bash, and I was told by George that I was allowed 20 minutes to present any new materials for approvals. I told him that I needed more time, but he said 20 was all I was allowed.

I was scheduled to make my presentation after a board member who was the marketing expert made his presentation. As he did not have much to offer, he suggested that I make my presentation first and that he would make his comments afterwards. My 20 minutes became 45 minutes, and upon completion, all of my new materials were approved.

You can't win them all but this time my score was 100%. Don't think that you will always win sometimes you win a bunch in a row and then lose a few .Don't let your ego get too high or too low.

The 100% win was the result of what I had learned from my experiences and the School of Hard Knocks. Never assume that people have more knowledge or abilities than you do.

Lessons learned:

 The biggest impediment to success in my career was mostly other people and on occasion me. It's how we learn to deal with them that are important. I learned that sometime you can't control the way you feel but you need to control the way we act.

Chapter 30

Trust yourself; you know more than you think you do. Dr. Spock

The 20th anniversary dinner was something else with both sides patting themselves on the back over the success in helping families prepare for their children's future post- secondary education. It was a beautiful black tie dinner with speeches and both sides praising themselves for the wonderful achievement over the past 20 years even though they had yet to make a dent in a huge market not yet tapped, parents waiting to learn about the opportunity to prepare for their children's education.

After a cocktail party, dinner with first class wine and after- dinner drinks, both side parted.

I don't know where the foundation staff and board members went, most likely back home to the comfort of their beds, but not the marketing group.

I was to learn one of George's methods of communicating and socializing with the Enrolment Directors was what he called the "EAGLE'S NEST". The Eagle's nest was a suite at the Inn on The Park Hotel stocked with as much booze as the average liquor commission outlet. It was open from just after dinner until sun-up and those still standing made it back to their rooms. I guess this was the way things were done in the old insurance days; god, I hope not.

With today's "0" tolerance, the cops would have had a field day.

Discussions turned into debates and debates into arguments about deficiencies in home office administration and lack of sales by the Enrollment Directors. It was an eye opening experience as was my first meetings with the total field sales force. I will never forget my first encounter in Vancouver with John Papp and Dick Gleig where I was tagged as another home office idiot.

I had prepared all my new marketing materials in mechanical form and tacked them on the walls of the suite. There was a new mall display with graphics on full display for all to see, and I awaited their reactions.

The first to react were the two Directors from Vancouver who grabbed me and ushered me out onto the patio, out of earshot of George and the other Directors. The first words out of their mouths were that they owed me an apology, that I was not a home office idiot but one of them. I didn't know if this was a compliment or not. They said they had asked for a new brochure and I had given them the tools to make us a ton of money and the ability to reach more families with our message of hope for their children's future education.

George had suggested that what the field needed was maybe a new brochure this year and something else next year and maybe something else the following year. This meant the materials that I had developed would cover my work for the next ten years as I had developed ten new marketing tools all in one shot. The most important tool that was needed was a sales training program to teach all Enrollment Directors and agents to follow a uniform home office approved sales methods. George felt it was not needed as the old insurance methods that he was brought up with were good enough. So even though I had partly completed a new sales manual, it was not approved, so I put it on the shelf.

My manual later proved was what was needed and would have saved the company many problems over the years with the various Securities Commission. More about that later.

My job was then to become a social director, visiting with the Enrollment Directors, having a short meeting, long lunches and expensive dinners and lots of booze. I could see why one could become an alcoholic or maybe even suffer from gout from all this fine food.

The success of my new marketing materials and abilities soon became known to the then competitors, and I received a call from the new owner of University Scholarships, a Mr. Bill Graham who invited me to dinner. I told George McQuat about the invitation, and he had no problem with me meeting the competition. Having no idea what Mr.Graham had in mind, I agreed to meet with him.

I was to learn that he had recently purchased the marketing rights and the foundation's scholarship plan from Morguard Trust that had been managing the trust for several years after the marketing arm was closed down by the original owners that I had sold plans for in mid 1965.

 Over dinner and a few drinks and a lot of conversation, he asked if I would consider becoming a partner in his business as he needed help in developing and managing a sales force as well as my marketing skills.

Here I was having just started working with Canadian American and now with an offer to partner with the competition. I told him that I would have to do some serious brainstorming and would get back to him. We met again a week later, and he offered me 40% of the business for $67,500 dollars investment. Now, I had some serious thinking to do and needed help in evaluating his offer, so I had my lawyer and accountant do their due diligence. What we discovered that he was way underfunded to finance any growth and that my investment would not be sufficient to grow the business. I decided to decline his offer which was probably the worst decision I had made to date.

He found a silent partner that co- signed with the bank to advance commissions to the agents and found a sales manager to help build the business, and his business started to grow. We kept in contact over the next few years and in some way became somewhat friends.

In the meantime, sales increased with Canadian American, and the agencies were doing well under my management.

Up to this point, I managed to remain sober but started to have second thoughts about my future with this company.

Lessons learned:

What I experienced for the second time in the corporate world was how power goes to some executive's heads and ultimately works its way down their anatomy making them act like super studs which leads in many cases to their ultimate downfall. Alcohol is the next biggest problem in the corporate world due to all the pressures of running a business. Being in a position above your abilities and ending up incompetent is probably the worst position to be in. Make sure you have the knowledge to perform at that level or you're doomed for failure.

Chapter 31

You are never too old to set another goal or dream a new dream.   C.S. Lewis

Two years disappeared, and I felt it was time to take a break from the pressures of managing a direct sales force which I had been involved up to this point in my life some 25 years. Another reason was if I remained in this atmosphere with George and John Atkins and the long liquid lunches, I could possibly become a raving alcoholic—a Jew and a raving alcoholic was few and far between but still possible. I felt it was time for a break and new challenge.

My son Aron was studying at Trinity College and was sharing an apartment with another young man from Montreal. He suggested that on our next trip to Montreal we meet his roommate's parents. We met for dinner, and this young man's father asked what high school I attended. I told him Baron Byng, and he said he attended it as well. We talked about some of the things we did, and he said that one day he threw ink out the window of his classroom on someone's car. This had happened 30 years ago, and I told him that it was my car. He was so embarrassed in front of his wife and son that he picked up the tab for dinner. What goes around surely comes around; sometimes it takes a while.

Shortly after, I asked George McQuat for a leave of absence and off to Winnipeg I went. I decided to take the leap and commit my time and money with no safety net, forfeiting all the benefits of security, medical insurance and guaranteed income, some of the benefits of working for a corporation.

 I had a dream that this was something I wanted to do and made the commitment. I felt that I needed to commit my full time to my side business if it was to succeed and become profitable.

My investment in Ultralight aircraft was not a large one but was at a point that needed some marketing skills. Here I was facing a new challenge knowing nothing about flying or manufacturing airplanes. Starting a new business was not easy especially in a new industry.

My creative juices started to flow, and I quickly developed a plan to open Ultralight Flight Centres where we would teach would- be pilots to fly these aircraft which was becoming more and more popular. A new recreational sport was evolving as man has always had a dream of flight, and learning to fly an Ultralight was as close as one could get.

Being a whole new industry, several manufactures in the USA were selling kits that would be pilot would have to assemble. Assembly manuals were poorly written with even poorer illustrations which made it very difficult if not almost impossible to assemble properly. The result was an accident waiting to happen, and it did happen too many times.

At that time, no license was required to fly Ultralights, so untrained pilots went up and then down some sustaining serious injuries and or death " No one ever was injured or died while in the air…it was that sudden impact with the ground that was the problem."

The budding industry need to improve its image to make learning to fly safe or at least safer. So I put my thinking cap on and made a list of what was needed. First needed was an Ultralight flight training manual and second proper flight instruction and third properly illustrated assembly manuals.

To help with all this, I brought in a new partner with experience in the aeronautical field in design and assembly. Paul Pytel was the man, and he quickly developed assembly manuals that one could read and follow.

Next, we hired an experienced bush pilot as our test pilot and instructor. His job was to teach dealers and flight instructors the art of flying these aircraft. The next big job was to develop and write a flight training manual with illustrations similar to regular flight training manuals but simple enough that anyone could follow.

Here it became my challenge. I had flown an Ultralight a few times but had never taken a flight training program. All I really knew was what goes up must come down,in that order. So, a new learning skill was needed and quickly. I did research on what was covered in regular pilot training to obtain a pilot's license and did an outline of what I considered important for the would be Ultralight pilot.

I hired an illustrator and started writing what was to become one of the first training manuals.

When it was completed, I presented it to the M.O.T. in Ottawa who were now looking at introducing some form of licensing requirements for Ultralights as there were more and more accidents happening with the growing popularity of the sport. M.O.T. approved my manual.

This was what we needed to move to the next step which was setting up dealers to operate and teach would- be dreamers of flight to fly like an eagle. We came up with the brand for the centers, "Adventure Flight Centers" and our brand of Ultralights named the "Skyseeker."

It was a simple business concept where if you enjoyed flying and the new sport of Ultralight flight and were willing to learn how to instruct others, we would offer you a territory to operate an Adventure Flight Center.

A dealer would pay a fee for the rights to the territory which included two Ultralights, some spare parts and flight manuals and flight instruction to become certified and you were in business.

For someone who wanted to learn to fly and possibly own their own Ultralight, it was relatively inexpensive compared to regular flight training or purchasing a regular airplane. You could learn to fly and own your own Ultralight for about $4,000 dollars.

Many of our first Adventure Flight centers were farmers who already knew how to fly or always wanted to learn. They had the land and existing buildings, and this was something they could do in their off seasons.

The first model Ultralights were swing seat versions with cables that controlled the rudder by movement left or right and up and down movement for take -off and landing. For take- off, you would pull the seat forward until you achieved ground speed of 20mph and then swing back and the plane would lift off. Turning right or left, you would swing your body in either direction and the plane would turn. Glide ratio was 6-1 which meant that if the motor failed, you could glide quite a distance. In the early years, this sport became very popular because of the affordable price for the new would- be pilots. But as the cost of flying regular aircraft became more expensive, a new group of experienced pilots took to the sport. Having flown regular aircraft, they wanted additional features such as ailerons, stick shift control and rudder controls which increased the cost considerably.

 Other options were floats to take off from the lake and skis for winter then enclosures to protect from the wind and cold.

When we first started to fly the original models in Winnipeg which has to be one of the coldest spots in Canada, we flew at -35 degrees with no windshield. We wore a down filled mask and ski goggles which kept your face very warm but fogged-up your ski goggles. To correct this, we would breathe thru a snorkel. It really was a fun sport.

Airline pilots and famous stars took up the sport. John Denver took to the sport and not only sang at the Oshkosh air show but also flew an Ultralight. He later died while flying an experimental aircraft in California.

I no longer dreamt of seeing man fly; I was watching it happen every day.

Chapter 32

Don't worry about failures, worry about the chances you miss when you don't even try.

We were now into our third year of manufacturing and with Flight Centres in operation in several provinces. The demand for more features from a new growing group of licensed pilots created a need to redesign and retool which was a costly investment that we could not afford at the time.

To what we thought and believed would be our savior, the Manitoba Government introduced a grant program to help developing businesses. We applied and were told that our business qualified and that we should make application and that we would soon receive funding to retool and design new models.

We hired an aeronautical engineer to help Paul Pytel with the structural design that would have to be approved by M.O.T. before we could retool and start to manufacture.

In the meantime, my job was to work with the Gov't to obtain the grant. I met with the head of a new department set up to oversee the distribution of funding. The Manitoba Gov't had set up new offices to support the program with offices and equipment to support about 50 new employees. When I first entered the new building, it was staffed with no more that 3 civil servants. Advertising promoting this new exciting program was in every newspaper, and I'm certain that the Gov't spent several million dollars promoting it.

After going through all the steps and completing all the paperwork required, I was told we would have the funds we needed quickly. Not having dealt with government before I trusted what I was told. Weeks became months and still no funding, so I decided to meet with the Minister overseeing the program and when we met he acted shocked that the process was taking so long. He put me in touch with his Deputy Minister and when I explained my frustrations to him he stated that the problem was the "stupid civil servants" that were to blame and that he would meet with the finance committee the following Tuesday, and we would have our grant and funds quickly. Weeks again became months of more bullshit.

By this time, we had spent all of our cash developing the new models and had no dollars for retooling and purchase of new raw materials. I was one angry puppy and decided I would meet with the Deputy Minister one last time. I booked an appointment for 4.30 the following day, and when I went to his office, his secretary told me he was just on the phone and would meet with me shortly. Fifteen minutes went by, then 30 minutes, and his secretary was becoming embarrassed with the delay and went into his office to find out when he would be free; he was not there. She said he probably went the john and would return soon. I waited another 30 minutes and was now fit to be tied after being jerked around for months and seeing our business quickly go down the tubes. On my way out, I decided to see if the Minister was still in his office and discovered that his office was attached by a short hallway from the Deputy Minister's and that he had left the building this way probably on his way to the closest bar.

I went home and decided that the next morning I would meet with a reporter from the SUN newspaper and tell my story. It was printed the next day, front page and included the comment from the Deputy Minister about the "stupid civil servants". I would not want to have been in his position that morning.

I decided that morning that it was time to pack my bag and leave Manitoba and never look back. I took the keys to our bank and told them the business was now theirs to do with as they pleased and back east I drove. The end of an interesting and challenging 3 years and an experience that I will never forget.

 It was also the final step in my so called marriage, and I applied for a final divorce in Winnipeg on the grounds of adultery, not mine, hers.

There is a saying in Winnipeg that in the winter the temperature drops to-30 degrees with a wind chill factor of 30 miles per hour…you can freeze your skin in 30 seconds. It's called 30/30/30. When I would tell friends or business associates about this, they would as who would want to live there, and I would tell them there is a definite benefit. They would ask what that could be and I would say that the cold stops the aging process and that I was not 51 but 85. The women would immediately jump up and say they were moving to Winnipeg.

Another chapter in my varied careers chalked-up. Another notch in my belt from the School of Hard Knocks. There comes a point in a business or personal situation where you have to accept reality do not let your ego control your decisions, make the best decision and move on.

Chapter 33

Not knowing what my next career move would be, I needed some time to once again recharge my battery and reflect what the last 3 years had taught me.
After putting my belongs in storage and saying goodbye to my cat who I left with a neighbor, it was time to head east and visit with friends and family that I had not seen in 3 years.
First stop was Richmond, ON to spend some time with my friends John and Ingrid and their 2 children to whom I was unofficially an uncle as I had been part of their family since they both were adopted.
It was pleasant to be with them as we had become good friends over the years.
I had helped John obtain a position of Enrollment Director with University Scholarships in 1980, marketing scholarship savings plan "RESP'S" as Canadian American at the time did not have any openings.
His agency had become one of the top producers but most of the sales were produced by him personally.
One evening as we were sitting around the pool and enjoying a few drinks, the conversation centered on his agency, and he said that he was having problems hiring agents that would produce sales on a consistent basis.
I asked him to role play a typical presentation with the tools he used.
Ingrid and I played the role of the parents that needed to be convinced that we had to save for our children's future post-secondary education.
John's presentation was unique as he used only conversation to present the plan to us; even some of his words and sales techniques were something I felt were personal to him and would be difficult for others to copy and use. An example of words he used was that "we all have a dream of what we want our children to become a doctor a scientist a nurse or without a post- secondary education maybe a bartender or stripper". John could say this in his own unique way and not be insulting, but I did not think any of his agents could.
I took some notes and my creative juices began to flow on how I could turn some of his unique ideas into a presentation anyone could follow.
Later that evening after dinner, we were back sitting around the pool and having another drink. The conversation turned to what Ingrid was doing in the agency, and she said she was helping with some of the paperwork.

I sensed some frustration and unhappiness with her role as John was not organized with minor details such as keeping proper records. Typical of sales agents good at sales but lousy at minor details and paperwork.

I asked her what she would like to do and suggested that maybe she would be happier working out of the home. She replied that she had been out of the workforce for over 10 years and had no idea what she could do. I felt that her earning some of her own income would make her happier and more secure as I knew there were problems with their marriage because of John's drinking which she informed me had become worse with the pressures of running his agency.

I suggested that maybe she should become an agent and earn her own income, and she felt that she did not have the confidence to sell anything and that she could not explain the plan like John.

I said what if there was a presentation that she could follow not using John's words would she be willing to give it a try. She still was not sure that she could sell anything, being a little shy and over the years of marriage short on personal confidence.

The next day we worked on putting together a presentation flip chart and Educational Survey, something I had done several times before for Famous Artist Schools and ICS.

Ingrid did some artwork and a few charts, and I put all the words together, and by the end of the day, we had a visual presentation that now could be used by all of John's agents.

 Ingrid was impressed, so I asked her if she would be able to do a presentation using the new materials. She made the mistake of saying she could, and that's when I challenged her to give it a try. She was afraid to go out on a call on her own, so I arranged for my son Aron to go with her for support. I wanted her to try it without my help to prove to herself that she could do it on her own. The result on her first presentation was she made her first sale and earned over $700 dollars.

This first sale was a life changing event for her and over the next several months, I saw her confidence and self esteem blossom.

It was July of 1985 and time to start investigating my next career move. It was also time for me to step back and reflect what I learned up to this point in my life. I felt I needed time to wind down before deciding my next career challenge.

Chapter 34

Life is like a roller coaster, live it ,be happy, enjoy life. Avril Lavigne

While I was in Winnipeg, Bill Graham and his sales manager Dean Madsen had kept in touch and offered me the position of agency director to manage Manitoba and Saskatchewan which at the time I refused as I felt I needed all my time to develop my Ultralight business. George McQuat also kept in contact and told me that anytime I wanted to rejoin Canadian American, I would be more than welcome.

So now I had some soul searching to do; was I interested in going back into the scholarship business or move on to other opportunities? After weeks of weighing the pros and cons, I decided that I should at least hear what they both had to offer. George invited me to visit his home for Saturday lunch time and sit around the pool where we could discuss his offer of employment, away from the office. So down the 401 I went and spent an interesting afternoon being updated on what had been happening with the company over the past 3 years. My development of all the marketing materials had help increase sales considerably while I was in Winnipeg. George outlined his offer of employment which I found somewhat confusing, so I asked him to put it in writing so I could review it over the next week and get back to him. He agreed to send it to me early the following week, and we scheduled another lunch the for the following Saturday.

I decided that I should also meet with Bill Graham on Friday and see what he had to offer before meeting with George again.

So back down the 401 for another lunch meeting. Bill explained that he had filed a prospectus in Quebec as this was the only province that he was not licensed in. He told me that he had hired a sales manager for Quebec, and I asked what this individual's background was. He told me that his name was Bob Kouri and that he was a retired high school principal, a funny choice for a sales manager with no sales experience. We finally got around to discussing what role he was prepared to offer me.

I was confused as his offer was sales manager for Quebec, the same position that he already hired Bob for. I asked him why he thought he needed two sales managers and his response was that Bob had contacts with the Liberal government and the School boards and was fluent in French. An obvious benefit, and with my sales background, we would make a good team.

My first impression was that as a start-up in Quebec, it would take time to create acceptance and recognition of the plan in Quebec and that to make it work I would need authority to develop sales and marketing tools geared for this bilingual market. My previous sales experience in Quebec would also be a big asset. As it would take some time to produce sales and that it would limit my income and bonuses for the first few years, I said I would have to think about his offer and get back to him.

So, the next morning I was back poolside with George McQuat I had time to review his offer that he had put in writing. I found I was even more confused with the terms of his offer now that I had a chance to read and review it.

His offer was salary and bonuses for first year, but in the second and following years, 80% of the past year's production would become the base for calculating bonuses the following year. This would mean that to earn the same income, I would have to produce 180%. I asked him who had come up with this idea, and his answer was this was the company's new policy to ratchet the numbers.

I told him that I thought that this new plan was rat shit rather than ratchet, and under these conditions, I would not be interested in rejoining the company.

So now if I was interested in going back into the scholarship business, I would have to consider Bill Graham's offer.

Bill called me a few days later, and I told him that the only way that I would be interested was if he extended his offer to include all of the Maritime Provinces. He agreed, and it was back to my old home town. This made it the second time since I left in 1967 after the FLQ decided to put bombs in mailboxes and started the first exodus of Anglophones out of the province. The second time was as V.P of sales for ICS in 1975. My exodus in 1967 was free as the company paid for my move, unlike many others who gave up everything just to get out of Quebec.

To this day, I still can't comprehend what stupidity that motivates the separatists to want out of Canada. I was born in Quebec and enjoyed the various cultures that made up the population, and we all managed to live in somewhat harmony.

So on to a new challenge back in the city of my birth. I was going back to where my selling career started but with decades of more sales and management skills, having worked all over Canada, the USA and England. Funny how sometimes what "goes a around comes around" and ends up back where you started.

Chapter 35

Success is the result of perfection, hard work, learning from failure, loyalty and persistence.

Colin Powell

It was now September of 1985, and it was 5 years since I left Montreal only to return once again. I had returned from the USA in 1975 and left again in 1980.
So onto my new challenge. I assumed that Bill had opened an office and was ready to start building a sales force boy was I in for a surprise. This was a complete start-up from scratch .I saw the challenges ahead but with my past business experiences and life skills I would be able to handle with no big problem.
I had learned all the special skill sets needed for this new challenge. For starters lease an office, purchase equipment design marketing materials and hire and train new agents and managers.
There are some people that are good at maintaining things and some that excel at starting things. In life you have to determine what your forte is. I knew mine was starting and building as maintaining was not one of my strong points as I would get bored quickly. My choice was to start, build and before getting bored move on.
I met Bob Kouri who had leased a business office 10x10 with one desk and that was how we started the Quebec operation.
Bill had filed a prospectus with the Securities Commission in Quebec, and it was returned for changes and clarification several times. The lawyers who prepared it were not familiar with the scholarship business and needed assistance on how to properly explain the features of the plan. Here is where my past experience in the scholarship business and writing enrollment agreements for ICS helped me to clarify features of the plan and rewrite the prospectus in a language that could be understood by members and the Securities Commission.
The process in dealing with the Quebec Securities Commission like any other Government office was a lengthy one that took almost a year from the first filing to finally get approvals. We finally received final approval the day before Christmas 1985.
Not knowing when and with what other changes the Securities Commission would require made life a difficult waiting period. I started preparing all the marketing

materials needed in mechanical form ready for printing and easy to make corrections if required by the Securities Commission.

Bob Kouri and I started recruiting and training agents even though we did not know when our prospectus would be approved. It had now been close to a year when the original had been filed.

One of the first agents that was hired was a Russian lady named Yeta Shteyn who was working as a substitute teacher teaching French and who's spoken English had a heavy Russian accent. I had trouble understanding her and wondered how she would be able to present the plan to Anglophones.

She was probably the only agent whose training lasted over 4 months while we waited for final approval. She learned the plan backwards, sideways and every feature in such detail that even Bill Graham would have been hard pressed to compete with her. She later told me that she had memorized the English presentation and would practice while driving to an appointment.

While waiting, we hired and trained several more agents, and I continued to prepare all the materials we need to start marketing. Developing a training manual and sales support materials was easy as I had done this several times before.all it needed was some adjustments.

Final approval came 1 day before Christmas, and the first thing we needed was enrollment applications printed. Bob had a friend in the printing business with whom I had been working with to prepare mechanicals, and he agreed to print the applications over Christmas.

We now had our applications; all we needed was a sale to kick off the Quebec operation. I had had a muffler replaced on my car a week before and talking to the owner had talked about our plan and found out he had a child of 2 years old. I decided to go see him, and he became our first member. We were now officially in business.

At the time, there were three other competitors in Quebec offering RESP plans. One was The Canadian Scholarship Trust (CST)   Heritage and the other Universitas. We had to be more innovative in our marketing to capture a share in this new market for us.

I designed a school information package to be distributed to the schools for the students to take home to their parents explaining the importance of saving for the children's Post Secondary Education which included a pamphlet requesting more information which the students were to return to the school.

Here is where Bob Kouri's past career as a high school principal came in big time. He and I worked with the school boards and principals to obtain permission to distribute these information packages. This was our first success at marketing and beating out the competition.

We were becoming visual in the marketplace, and this helped in our recruiting efforts. We had agents from the competitors contact us looking at the possibility of joining our team,

One such agent was a young man who had been promised to be promoted to District manager with CST and was being taken advantage by the enrollment director. His name was J.F. Nehme with the J being for Jean and the F for Francois.

He started with us as a district manager but very quickly became an enrollment director, building his own sales team.

Success came rapidly for him as he became one of our top producing enrollment directors and he quickly learned to follow my sales procedures and training. J.F. and I became friends right from the start, and today over 30 years later still manage to talk to each other at least once a week.

The old saying "do as I do" practiced by many managers does not work as no two people have the same personally or communication skills .To be successful you need to learn and follow a uniform presentation method using your own personality.

Chapter 36

Life is really simple, but we insist on making it complicated.   Confucius

Here I was back in Montreal, single and with a new challenge to build a new sales organization in Quebec and the Maritime provinces and far enough from home office and the pressures of office politics on a daily basis.

I had moved up to Ste. Saveur to the same house that I had leased for the winter when I was served with separation papers in 1977. Life was good: work all day and each night go back to god's country enjoying peace and quiet. Also finally becoming a part time ski bum a few nights and weekends. My skiing improved, and I finally made it to level 3 expert.

My love life also started to improve, and at one point. I was dating 3 different women at the same time, born again after 19 years of a lousy marriage. My work schedule was easy to manage, but my social life became more difficult as the months flew by. At Christmas and New Year, it was short of a disaster trying to keep track with whom, when and where I was supposed to be.

I kept in touch with John and Ingrid weekly and when the kids heard that I was skiing every weekend, they asked if they could come visit and learn. I decided that I would take one of them at a time before Christmas and the other at another time. Erin got the first opportunity and her Christmas gift from uncle Norton was skis and boots.

She was 11 years old and Ingrid and John put her on a train and I would pick her up in Dorval. I think I was more nervous than she was that she would arrive safely. But she did, and when she got off the train, this beautiful little lady was all excited and ready to learn a new skill. So off we went to a sports store to get her fitted with her first pair of skis and boots.

We arrived at the house after 9 p.m., and she wanted to try her new outfit so out we went and practiced walking and climbing the hill beside the driveway to get the feel of what to do.

 The next morning, we were up early and first on the hill practicing walking up and down the beginner's hill. I then signed her up with an instructor for a 2 hour lesson.

It was amazing how much she learned in those 2 hours as she was able to turn, snow plow and even stop. So after a break for lunch, we skied the balance of that day, and she was able to follow me, falling only a few times.

The next morning, we were back on the hill, and at noon, Ingrid was to meet us to take her back home. She had in one short day graduated from the beginner's hill to following me down hill 69 which was intermediate. At noon, when we reached the last crest on the hill, she spotted Ingrid, and I told her to follow me down making wide circles and no falling to impress her Mom.

The look on Ingrid's face was something to see, and she decided then and there if Erin could do it she would take some lessons and join the fun. Another ski bum was born that day.

I had made arrangements to spend the afternoon with one of my new lady friends who was an expert skier. She arrived 1 hour too soon, and I introduced her to Ingrid and noticed that Ingrid was not pleased to meet her. Stupid me; I then realized that her feelings for me were more than just being good friends.

That Christmas and New Year had me evaluating my relationships with my three ladies, and for some reason, I compared them with Ingrid. They all lost, and I realized then we were destined to become more than friends.

Here she was; my friend's wife, a difficult situation for sure. Their marriage was falling apart due to his drinking, and Ingrid was becoming more confident in her ability to support herself and the children as she was now an enrollment director building her own team. She had asked John if she could report to me directly and not be part of his team and that meant she would have to attend my weekly training and meetings in Montreal.

Over the next several months, their marriage became unlivable as John was drunk more than he was sober. They finally decided to live apart, and Ingrid moved one block away with Erin, Dan remained with John. This move so close was not a good idea and after a few months Ingrid decided to move to Montreal and rented an apartment in my building. My son and I helped them move. Here I was living on the 1st. floor with them on the third; Erin could not understand why I was not living with them.

 John and Ingrid were now officially separated and soon divorced, and he moved back to the states and reunited with his first wife. Life has a funny way of making things happen.

I subleased my apartment and moved upstairs to be with my two girls and their dog named Shadow, the start of what was to be the best relationship and first true love of my life.

We both had past issues to deal with to find a way of dumping our previous baggage, and a friend and business associate Francine recommended a program she thought would help. It was called the " Forum". Up to this point in my life, I had built walls around me to protect me from being hurt, and if anyone got too close, I would just build another wall in front of the other. This is what I had carried all my life, and it was time to try and dump it if I was to experience a true and lasting love, something that had eluded me up to this point in my life.

The" Forum" was a watered down version of what was offered in the states called EST. It lasted 5 days from 8am to midnight. There were 125 people attending with one moderator. He would choose a victim and challenge his/her thoughts by asking questions that finally got him/her to open up and talk about their problems. You would not believe some of the issues different people had to deal with in their lives. There were situations such as rape, loss of a mother or father through divorce, witnessing the accidental shooting of a family member to admitting you were gay.

I sat there for those 5 days and finally realized that my problem of trust was in fact not my problem at all …it was my mother's and father's issues, and I had been given the task of carrying it as my own.

During the program, we learned that when we are born our parents give us a lifetime present; that is a knapsack filled with all their shit, and we carry that for a lifetime. We also learned that it was really not ours to carry as we would fill our bag with our own crap and did not have to carry those of our parents. It was time to dump the bag.

The experience made me recall an old story that I heard years before. "The head Rabbi in Israel was on his deathbed and 2 young scholars took all of their savings to travel to the town where the Rabbi was, to ask him a question, only to end up in a line over two blocks long . They were concerned that by the time they got to his bedside it would be too late to get their question answered. They came up with an idea, why not pass their question down the line to whoever was with the Rabbi would ask their question which was" WHAT IS LIFE", the Rabbi getting weaker by the minute when asked said "LIFE IS A RIVER", the answer flowed back up the line to the scholars who did not understand the Rabbi's answer so back down

the line to the person with the Rabbi who said that the students did not understand his answer…the Rabbi weaker said ..”SO LIFE IS NOT A RIVER!”
 What wisdom…life is what you make it. It has to be your life, not your parents or anyone else.
What we also learned was life is nothing more than a conversation .It's what's happening right now, as yesterday is gone and tomorrow has not arrived yet. Learn to live life for the moment.
I dumped my crap and decided to tear down my walls and trust my relationship with Ingrid 110%.
 We were already best friends, and I today believe for a relationship to last you must first become best friends.
Here I was 53 year old and experiencing my first true love.

Chapter 37

Any action is better than no action at all. Norman Peale

It was now 1987, and in those 2 years that seemed to have flown by, the office was doing great with several Enrollment directors building their teams both in Quebec and all the Maritime provinces. New agents were being recruited weekly, and our sales volume was increasing week by week.

My responsibility was sales and marketing; the office was run by an office manager who reported to Toronto's office manager Caryn Taylor. The problem we were having was a backlog in processing welcome packages documents for the new members. We were several months behind as we were processing and printing every document by hand.

I kept asking Toronto for a solution, and the answer I got was they were working with their accounting firm to do a study of what we needed to solve the problem. As I had learned in the past, studies do not solve problems…solutions do.

So, I had to seek a solution as my agents were getting complaints from members and losing some sales because of the delays.

The solution came believe it or not on hill 69 in Ste.Sauveur while skiing. Dan had met a young girl on the hill, and when we stopped for lunch, she introduced me to her father who was working on his computer. I asked him what work he did, and he said he was a computer programmer. I told him about our problem, and he offered to see if he could find a solution. We met in my office on Monday, and he agreed to develop a program complete with a computer and printer for $3500 dollars. This was not my area of responsibility, but I gave him the go ahead anyway.

Within a week, he developed a program, and we tested it, and it solved our problem. We were able to print all documents for all new enrollments sold each week in 1 day and then catch up on the backlog.

A few weeks after the system was up and running, Bill Graham the big boss and Caryn Taylor arrived for their quarterly visit and review and happened to see the computer setup next to my office. They both asked who authorized its purchase, and Caryn said she had not. They said they were still doing a study and asked who authorized the purchase. I said I did, and they stated that this was not my area of responsibility. I said that it was and that the computer was mine as I had personally paid for it and that I did not need their permission. Bill and Caryn were pissed; I said I would show them something after 3p.m. as the only one who knew how to use the system was the programmer's 13 year old daughter who would be at our office after school.

Boy was I having fun with this situation and ultimately the solution to our problem. The demonstration took place at 3:30, and in less than 5 minutes, a complete welcome package was printed. Bill and Caryn's eyes lit up and I then said that this solved the problem that you have been studying for over 6 months and have probably paid some consultant thousands of dollars with no result. If you want to purchase the computer and system, I expect a cheque next week, or I take it home. A cheque arrived in 2 days. We laughed about this situation even years later

Lessons learned:

The only way to solve a problem is to take action!

Chapter 38

Comedy is simply a funny way of being serious.   Peter Ustinov

The name of the game in sales is recruit, recruit and that is what we did weekly. One ad we had placed in the French paper brought in a newly landed immigrant from France whose name was Philippe Jorajuria who spoke only French, not Quebec French but pure French which was hard for even a Quebecker to understand. He spoke no English, and I wondered if he would be able to present the plan properly even in French. His was determined he said to learn, and I decided to him a chance. First, he would have to do some marketing by distributing brochures to produce leads of interested families and then learn how to present the plan. He was a quick learner and even his few words of broken English improved quickly.

Every morning, he would go to newsstands and stores and insert a brochure in various newspapers as he could not afford to pay for any marketing. It produced leads constantly, and he, believe it or not, made sales and became a top producer. He even made sales to Anglophones by letting them read the presentation. On a group skiing trip to Morin Heights, a romance blossomed between him and another agent Francine Bureau, and they soon married and later adopted 2 beautiful children from China.

Dean Madsen was the V.P. of sales for Canada, and I reported to him, and we became friends. He was originally from England and still retained a bit of his British accent. His management style was somewhat unique and most of it took place in fine restaurants with many a bottle of fine wine. I thought he was a connoisseur but found out differently. I purchased a wine course, studied and was able to read labels and tell which region the different type of wines came from as well as the type of grapes grown in each region. So one evening when we were meeting to discuss business, sipping some wine I picked up the bottle and read the label. With his British accent, he said no! No! You fool that's not how you tell a good wine. Somewhat confused, I asked how do you choose a good wine, and he said you look at the menu and you choose the most expensive. So much for expense accounts. I'm sure Bill Graham had a bird every time he saw Dean's expense reports..

Chapter 39

The only difference between a good day and a bad day is your attitude.   Dennis S. Brown

In my day, living with someone who you thought was your soul mate was not a common practice as it is today. If I had had such a trial, my first marriage would have been over in a matter of weeks.

Living with Ingrid and Erin before making the big decision was the best thing that ever happened as we grew closer with each passing day, and I knew that this was the woman I wanted to spend the rest of my life with.

Funny how things happen that are right in front of our noses and we can't even see them. Erin told me that she and her brother when they were young saw their mother's happiness when I visited and said to each other that Mom should be with Uncle Norton. I guess it was meant to be even before we knew it.

We rented a cottage in Ste.Sauveur for the year for skiing and as a summer getaway and spent every weekend enjoying our new life and love.

I never enjoyed living in an apartment and started looking for a place in the country but close enough to the office. One Sunday, I saw a small ad for a home to rent in St.Lazare on an estate. I drove out to take a look and viewed an abandoned ranch home with a 3 car garage and attached 4 stall stable.

When I say abandoned, the front door was swinging open, the toilet was on the front lawn, the taps from the sinks were missing, light fixtures gone; what a shame for such a beautiful property to be left in. The property was a total of 100 acres with a ranch house and a tennis court. I was totally confused and thought I had gone to the wrong place.

The owner was asking $2500 per month, and I was sure it could not be for this disaster.

I did not tell Ingrid or Erin about it but decided I would try and find out what had happened here as this place properly fixed up would be what I was sure we would all enjoy.

I called one of our suppliers who lived in St.Lazare to see if he knew anything about it and he referred me to a friend who was a real estate agent in the area. The original owner had died and left the property to his 3 daughters from his first marriage. The second wife went ballistic and destroyed the place when evicted. This was like something out of a movie.

I thought about the property for a few days and what it would take to make it livable again. I then called the daughter who listed the property for rent and proposed that I would do the repairs if she agreed to pay for materials needed and offered to pay $1,000 a month not $2500 asked. To my surprise, after talking to her sisters she agreed.

I then told Ingrid and Erin, and they wanted to see it immediately. We drove out that night, and they fell in love with the place and a few short weeks later we moved in.

While we were cleaning up and doing repairs, we decided to take a break on Saturday afternoon and went to a horse auction in Huntingdon, Qc. Ingrid fell in love with a big quarter horse, and I with an appaloosa gelding. We got caught up in the bidding, and by the end of the day, we had ourselves two more mouths to feed. We brought them to their new home and let them run around in the paddock. Shadow, our lab, was watching from outside the fence having never seen a horse and decided this was fun and decided to run with them. She ran in-between their feet and got hit in her head, and by the time we found a vet, she had died. A happy time turned into a sorrowful loss of a beautiful dog.

Ingrid's horse Prince was sired by Impressive which was a famous race horse, but we found that he had been abused and would not let the Ferrier lift his hind feet for shoeing. It took many months of loving care for him to trust Ingrid to be able to lift his feet, and when it was shoeing time, she had to lift and hold his feet so he could be trim and shoes reset his shoes..

My appaloosa was another story, and I should have known just by his name "Sky Rocket Red" that his name meant something. After a few weeks getting used to the place, I figured it was time to take him for a test ride. So I saddled him up and climbed into the saddle and was immediately airborne. I had me a bucking bronc. My friend the Ferrier Peter Stephenson recommended a neighbor who did some training to work with Ski Rocket Red.

This is how I met Ken Alexander and his wife Jennifer and their beautiful six month old daughter Lindsay.

Ken saddled up and the second his rear end hit the saddle he was airborne. He tried several time with the same result. It was a bucking bronc show. Luckily. No one was injured.

Jennifer asked Ingrid if she could try Prince, and we all were amazed at how well trained he was. She asked if she could enter him in a horse show in VanKleek Hill Ontario the following week, and this beautiful big boy took first place.

There was a riding stable close by so I went to talk to one of their trainers. I told him about Red, and he said that there wasn't a horse he could not ride and agreed to come over and work with Red that evening.

I called Ken, and we all watched what we thought would be a bucking bronc show. He just climbed into the saddle, and the horse did nothing. He rode him around and up and down the driveway, turning him with foot signals; we all stood there with our mouths open. I suggested he come back and try again tomorrow, and he agreed.

The next night was when the fun began. He saddled up and walked the horse out of the stable and jumped up onto the saddle and was immediately airborne, not just once but seven times before he got to the paddock.

I decided to call the previous owner in the USA, and he told me he had bought Red for a school horse and that he would always buck when you first mounted but after was so gentle a child could ride him.

I was too old for this exercise and decided to trade Red for something gentler.
One exceptional horse out of two was not a bad batting average.

A week later, I was riding a new quarter horse mare, and a few nights and weekends, we and the Alexander's would ride on the trails around St. Lazare.
Jennifer was afraid to take Lindsay their 6 month old daughter in a backpack so Uncle Norton rode with this beautiful little girl on his back giggling until she fell asleep.

That was 30 years ago, and we are still best friends. We became godparents to their second daughter Lauren Ashley Ingrid Holt Alexander. Note the addition of Ingrid's name.

Lessons learned:

Good friends are sometimes hard to come by so cherish them.

Chapter 40

Confidence come not from always being right, but from not fearing to be wrong. Peter T. Mcintyre

It was now the summer of 1988, and life was great. The office was doing well with sales increasing each and every week.

Ingrid's sales team was stable, and she was in her own right doing very well financially.

We decided it was time to make our relationship legal and planned our wedding to take place on the property. We tied the knot on August 27th. My long time friend and the brother I never had Joe was the best man, and Ingrid's sister Brigitte was the maid of honor. I thought I was the best man, not Joe.

It was a beautiful ceremony with family, friends and business associates all having a great time helping us celebrate.

It was time to get another dog, and we found a beautiful yellow lab that we named Sandy. When she was a few months old, we introduced her to the pool which became her favorite place to play. If we were in the pool, she would grab our wrist and pull us to safety. If we were sitting around the pool, she wanted us to jump in or throw her ball, and she would leap in a retrieve it. She became another family member until she passed away at age 14.

Sale production was up across the country and what normally happens with success is that it goes to our heads and here is where greed sets in. Bill decided to hire a consultant who knew nothing about our business to restructure management and systems.

Here's where stupidly sets in. We spent three days filling out tear sheets and plastered them all over the conference room. On the fourth day with all managers and Bill, we reviewed them and then did an exercise on our newly learned skills.

I was seated at the end of the conference table, and Bill pointed at me to start the discussion which was believe it or not "What business are we in." Wow... 4 days had led to this!

I decided to have some fun and said that I did not have an answer and he should start at the other end or the table and by the time it got back to me I would probably figure out an answer. Bill was pissed and not a happy camper with my answer.

Some of the answers from the other managers were that we were in the education business, in the financial service business, in the education funding business, in the savings business, a trust company, RESP providers etc.

What goes around comes around, and it was back to me. Bill, still pissed, asked me what business did I think we were in and here is where I shocked them all.

I said after these answers you probably don't want to hear my answer. If you think he was pissed at me before, it was getting worse by the minute.

I said that none of the above answers made any sense and unless we understood what business we were really in we would never become a leader in our industry.

Now, the whole group was pissed at me and were giving me dirty looks, probably saying what an idiot.

I then said that yes, today we are marketing RESPs, and I then picked up my coffee cup and said tomorrow we could be selling cups. They all looked at me trying to figure where I was going with my answer.

I said the truth is we are nothing more than a direct sales and marketing company. I then asked who was more important, our members or our agents. To this question, 70% said the members, and again I said wrong that it was our sales agents because without them there would be no members.

I listed some of the things we as a company had to do to support, motivate reward and recognize our sales agents and managers for sales achievements.

Boy, did I disturb the shit that day after 4 days of wasted time.

Bill listened and after some thought implemented everything I had suggested, and we were truly now a direct marketing company.

Before I stated that with success comes greed and sadly as well stupidity. The worst result that came out of that management meeting was that Bill took the advice of his expensive consultant and proposed a new regional managers' agreement that reduced our income. I told him that if he forced me to sign it I would resign. I said if this was the reward for a job well done he should rethink how he compensated us. His mistake was he thought my threat of resigning was an idle threat; boy, was he mistaken.

It was time to move on as I had never let anyone cut my income because of their greed. I always expected to be compensated based on my results, not that of some consultant.

What many companies don't understand is that they should never attempt to reduce the income of their employees that produce the results. He learned a lesson and went through several managers and never found one with my skills.

I was never afraid to move on to new challenges.

Chapter 41

In the end, we only regret the chances we didn't take, relationships we are afraid to have, and decisions we waited too long to make.

It was now August 1990, and I had been approached several times over the past several months by a businessman who wanted to start an RESP marketing company and Foundation. He said that he was consulting with Dean Madsen the previous sales V.P of USC and was looking for a sales manager to help set up the new organizations.

I had stated that I had not been interested on two or more occasions as I was happy with the position I had. He kept on trying to entice me with different offers each meeting. His final offer was 25% shares in the new company and a commitment to open internationally. This was now something to consider seriously.

I did not want to move to southern Ontario as we were happy living where we were, and, in fact ,we had purchased a beautiful ravine lot and decided on the style of home we were going to build.

Bill was in negotiation with Investors Group to sell the company, and he had to declare all existing contracts. While I was at home office, his partner Stu Ripley and the company accountant asked me if I had a management contract. I said yes, and Stu asked me for a copy; I said that he should ask Bill. He insisted that I fax him a copy which I did. Bill called me upset and angry and asked why I had sent it and I said your partner requested it; was there a problem?

For some reason, Bill did not want Investors to know that management contracts existed. Maybe this would have lowered the selling price. To me, it seemed that he was not protecting us, and this was another reason for me to rethink my future with this company.

Bill kept on trying to get me to sign a new agreement which I refused, and we decided to move on and accept the offer, a decision that did not come lightly.

It was a big move as we not only had to move our belongings but our 2 horses as well. I decided that if we were making all these changes I should probably trade in my mare for more of a show horse as Ingrid's Prince was show material.

Off to the horse dealer Paul Nightingale in Ste Sophie, Qc. I went every weekend trying different horses and not finding any better than what I already had. I was about to give up but decided to give it one last try. That day, I decided to take the horse trailer with me, just in case I got lucky in my search.

I tried another several horses that had arrived that week and again no luck. While talking to Paul, I was leaning against one of the stalls, and there was the most beautiful quarter horse I had ever seen. I looked at his papers and discovered he was only two and a half years old and probably not trained.

 Paul said he had just been transported yesterday and that he would take a look at his documents and see if he had any training. My luck: he had been green broke by a professional trainer in the USA so we decided to saddle him up and do a test ride. Paul mounted first, and we were surprised how gentle he was. I then rode him for about 45 minutes,he was nervous but pretty well behaved.

 I told Paul I would take him home to have veted, and if he was sound, we would make a deal on a trade with my mare that I had bought from him previously. He veted out with flying colors, and I had found my dream horse. He was fully registered with the American Quarter Horse Association and was sired by a famous father "Doc Bar". Boy, had I lucked in.

Lessons learned:

We packed up all our belongings, sold our dream lot and moved on to what we believed was a great opportunity. Moving on to new challenges was something I was able to do easily.

Chapter 42

Two things are infinite; the universe and human stupidity and I'm not sure about the universe. Albert Einstein

The gentleman and I use this term lightly as I was to learn more about his true character over the next several months. I was now partnered with whose name was Al Haid. He owned a religious book distribution business and several religious book stores in Ontario and Alberta. He claimed he was a millionaire and owned many commercial buildings which I found to be true when I had him checked out. What we did not find out that he was mortgaged to the hilt and was stealing from one business to try and keep the other alive. It was 1990, and real estate values had dropped considerably. His mortgages were up for renewal, and the lenders would only issue new mortgages based on the properties' current values. He was in the process of draining all his businesses to try and save his empire.
So a millionaire one day and close to Poverty Street the next.
He had worked with Dean Madsen preparing a prospectus and had filed it with the Securities Commission for approvals. When I read what they had put together, it was a copy of the University Scholarship Plan. I later found out that he had promised Dean that they would be partners in this new venture, something that he never had the intention of honoring. This was the first sign of his ethics.
I told him that if we went with the same plans as three other competitors we would have difficulty recruiting and selling against the competition.
What we needed was a new plan with better features and more flexibility than any of the existing plans that had been around for over 20 years with no changes.
At first, he did not want to make any changes as this would delay and approvals from the OSC. I finally wore him down, and since approvals were probably months away, he agreed.
He was busy trying to hold his failing empire together so it was up to Ingrid and me to set up the office, systems and rewrite the prospectus.

When we made our big move to our new home in Burlington, a friend and his wife drove down to help. Jean Francois (J.F.) was an enrollment director with USC that I had hired in 2006.

We all met with Haid and his wife for dinner, and he too was taken in by Haid bragging about being a millionaire that ultimately turned out to be a pile of bullshit.

We had both agreed in the past that the plans needed changes, and this was an opportunity to develop a new and superior plan. J.F. decided to join the team and help in its development.

First, we needed to rewrite the prospectus with some new features, and Ingrid had to set up the systems for the foundation and the distributor.

The Foundation we named "The Children's Education Trust of Canada and the distributer." Education Funds".

My title was International Executive Vice President, but as I was to learn,it meant nothing as Haid's true personality started to show. Even his commitment of 25% shares wasn't worth the paper it was printed on.

One of the biggest issues with the existing plans was the time allowed to be able to transfer the plan to another child. It was prior to age 17; this was called the year of eligibility. I felt that this was too early as the student in many cases did not know what career to study or if he or she wanted to pursue a Post Secondary education. The other was that if the student did not decide what course of studies to pursue before age 17, the scholarship funding would be lost.

To improve the plan, we changed the year of eligibility to age 21 and a new option called the Self determined option. This option gave the student the choice of pursuing a 1, 2 or 3 year program of studies. The only loss was the membership fees would be forfeited. If the student decided not to continue his education, the parents as subscribers would be refunded their savings and interest.

When I had proposed these changes to USC and even to Haid, they all said it would deplete to amount of money in the scholarship pools. I had to prove them wrong.

By extending the year of eligibility from age 17-21, the savings would add more interest to the pools and if students dropped out even more so. In fact, it did not harm the pools but enhanced them.

These and a few other features made the plan unique and better that all the others. It made it easier to sell and helped in recruiting agents from some of the other plans.

We finally received OSC approvals and now we're ready to start building a sales organization. We needed trading officers in each province as well.

Ingrid with the help of a computer specialist had the systems ready for the new members and for the sales agents.

I was busy recruiting all over Canada as was J.F. in Ontario. I appointed J.F. and Paul van Herten as Divisional directors for Ontario, and they were busy recruiting. We needed an Enrollment director in B.C., and I hired Lyndie Headley, a Jamaican who was working for one of the competitors in Edmonton and convinced him to move to a warmer climate in Vancouver.

I flew out to help him recruit and decided to have Ingrid join us for the weekend. I paid for her flight personally.

While I was away, J.F. and Paul had recruited a large team of agents and a Director from the competition and were busy arranging their transfer papers and training of our new plan.

Haid decided to interfere by offering them an office and having them report to him, not J.F., as the division director. He oversold them with crazy promises, and they lost trust in him and decided not to join us.

When I flew back on Sunday afternoon from Vancouver, J.F. picked me up at the airport and said that Haid had called him for a meeting that evening at a restaurant. He did not know I was back, and I decided to join him.

When we arrived, I saw that Haid was annoyed that I was there. He was with his wife and a guy I had been talking to about helping us with some marketing. They had had a few beers and the reason he wanted to see J.F. was to tell him that the director that J.F. had hired would not report to him but to Haid.

I said he could not do this as J.F. and Paul had exclusive rights as divisional directors for hiring in Ontario.

He answered that the hell with them; he could do whatever he wanted. Next, he spouted that my wife Ingrid was an asshole because she had the nerve to tell his wife before she flew to Vancouver to lock the file cabinets every night as they contained member files and commission records.

I almost jumped across the table and punched him but held back as you do not fight stupidity with stupidity. I then told him he was the asshole as he did not appreciate what Ingrid had accomplished and because of his foul mouth, that effective immediately Ingrid no longer worked for the company J.F. and I left before I would do something that I would maybe later regret.

This was the beginning of the end as I now saw Haid's true colors. He had no ethics and no honor, probably the worst type of individual that I had met or associated to date. He was a true con artist.

When Ingrid did not show for work on Monday, the shit hit the fan as she was the only one who knew how to process new members and pay commissions to agents. Haid called me into his office and had the nerve to ask her to give 2 weeks' notice and train someone to run the office. I told him after his insult that she would not step one foot into the office. I asked him to issue my shares and to get on with building the business. He refused so it was time for me to see a lawyer.

A friend recommended a lawyer, and when I explained my situation, he asked who this individual was. I told him Al Haid; he said, to my surprise, that scum bag. I then found out that Haid had been negotiating with another USC agency director Cheryl Lynch and her husband for months in bad faith.

This must have happened when I first refused his offer and when it went south with them is when he came after me again.

He suggested that we send Haid a letter requesting the immediate issue of my shares or that I would terminate my agreement with him.

Of course, the scum bag did not comply, so I emptied my desk and chalked this experience up as the worst decision of my life.

I had always believed that honesty and integrity were important in any business relationship. And when it's not there, move on.

When I look back at what we accomplished with the new plan features, it made me proud that I was finally able to make the plan more advantageous for parents to save for their children's education. Within a year, the other plans adopted these features. I remembered my grandmother's saying "the wheel turns and it will get back to the same spoke and you never have to push it." I'm sure that he would get his payback sooner or later.

We were living in Burlington, ON, and Erin was going to High School 1 block from our home. It was 1991, and we lived in fear for her as this was the time of the Paul Bernado and Karla Homolka abductions and murders of 2 young girls, Kristen French and Leslie Mahaffy. We would not let her walk to school alone. It was a fearful time for families in the area.

LESSONS LEARNED:

Never give up your ethics and your reputation for the almighty buck! In life it's fine to make mistakes and misread people. We can't learn everything about people and their character; you have to take the time to get to know what makes them tick and whether you want them in your life. Are they a positive or negative influence?

Chapter 43

My mission in life is to not only survive, but to thrive, and to do so with some passion, some compassion, some humor and some style   Maya Angelou

Free again, and time to recharge our batteries, so off to a 2 week trip to Mexico. We chose a hotel out of the way in a small cove right on the beach .It had a swim-up bar and a shack on the beach that served fresh shrimp and fish, brain food just that we needed after our ordeal with the Haids. We kayaked in the bay with porpoises in front and beside us, nature at its best.
We had no idea what we wanted to do, but we knew for sure we needed to take time to make the right decisions for our next career move. I had had enough of working for a company in management and dealing with all the home office politics. So, maybe it was time to try something else.
We looked into network marketing and became wellness consultants with Nikken selling magnetic mattresses and other health products and made it quickly to Silver level which is 4 up the volume ladder.
In a training session with Nikken, we were doing an exercise about goals and dreams and one exercise was we were asked to draw our dream. Ingrid was at one end of the room and me on the other. We were given some crayons and a tear sheet for this exercise
My drawing was a hobby farm with a pasture and stable with our 2 horses in the pasture. As an artist, I stink, and my picture looked like it was done by a six year old. Would you believe without any conversation between us Ingrid's drawing was the same as mine.
Ingrid's was a true work of art; the house looked like a house, the barn a barn, and the horses like horses. Each of us was then asked to show our dream, and when I showed my childish drawing, everyone laughed. When Ingrid showed hers, it was the same dream as mine but a work of art. We then were asked to set a goal when we wanted our dream to become a reality; we wrote down 6 months.
We decided that we could market these products anywhere, and we thought about moving back closer to family. We started to look around Ottawa where Ingrid's parents, sister and brother lived and close to Montreal where my sister lived. We

wanted a hobby farm as we still had our 2 beautiful horses. We had real estate agents all around Ottawa looking for properties and could not find what we were looking for that was in our price range.

 It was Mid June 1992, and we were driving to Montreal to meet with one of our distributors and stopped in Cornwall for gas and lunch and picked up a copy of the local newspaper. We had developed a habit of looking in all newspapers for hobby farm listings.

While I was driving Ingrid, read the paper and saw an ad listing for 7 hobby farms in Avonmore. I had no idea where this was so Ingrid looked at the map and said it was not too far from Cornwall. We called the agent and made an appointment to see the properties the next day.

The agents were a couple living in Avonmore on their own farm. When we arrived and after a bit of general conversation, the agents wife asked Ingrid about what type of a home we were looking for, an older home , a newer home, close to the road, off the road etc. Ingrid gave her answers, and she handed me a listing. I studied it and said that I don't think this one is for us. We then went to look at 6 other properties and did not see anyone that we liked. So, back to their farm to pick up our car and head back to Burlington.

The agent handed me back the first listing that she had given me and said we really should take a look. I said O.K. and that we would follow them with our car so we could make a quick getaway. The property was 5 minutes away from their home, and when we followed them into the driveway which was surrounded by trees for the first 150 feet, I stopped the car and before even seeing the house said to Ingrid that this was the place. Funny how I felt that this was our dream home, and we found it not in 6 months but in 3.

The property had a 3 story house and a separate building that was a two car garage and 63 acres of land, 8 clear and the balance trees and more trees. I had no idea how large 63 acres meant but when the agent told me the property was 600 ft. wide by over 4000 ft.deep, which is almost ¾ of a mile. WOW! We could not see the inside of the house as the listing agent was from Cornwall. We did not sleep that night as we were excited that we had found our dream home.

So, we made an appointment to view the house at noon the next day. When we arrived the agent opened the door and as we were about to enter he said that the property was sold. My heart sank, and I said why are you showing it then. He said there were conditions with the sale, and I asked what they were. He said that they had to sell their property first. I asked where their property was and what price were they asking. He said Cornwall and that their price was high and with over 20% unemployment at the time it would probably take some time to sell. They had 7 days to close if another offer came in.

Just at that point, my agent came out of the house and whispered to me that the accepted counter offer was sitting on the dining room table. In I went and read the offer and then we did an inspection of the property. The previous owner who was a Diplomat had died and had left the home fully furnished with European furniture to his stepson who lived west of Ottawa and who just wanted the cash.

The reason I did not want to see the property when the agent first handed me the listing was that the asking price was too low and every other property that we had seen with a low asking price was a piece of crap, next to a dump or next to another property with junk piled on their front lawns.

The asking price on the property was $89,000, and the accepted counter offer was $81,000.

We immediately went back to my agent's home and wrote up an offer for $ 83,000 with two conditions: that the roof was sound and that the well passed inspection. Closing was scheduled for August 15th as our lease in Burlington ended then.

A few days after our offer, other offers started coming in at over $100, 000, and I decided to take a chance and close immediately. Worst scenario was a new well and some roof repairs; we were not going to take a chance to lose our dream home. I called the lawyer and told him to close by Friday of that week. He said it couldn't be done, and I said nothing is impossible; just close on Friday. Ingrid and I loaded the horse trailer with everything we needed to start renovations and cleaning..The lawyer called back and said that the furnishings   had to be sold before closing, and I said they could hold an auction Saturday morning after closing.

We got the keys at 5:30 Friday and slept in sleeping bags that first night, happy that we had found our dream home for us and the Boys, our 2 beautiful horses who were still in Burlington.

Friday night, we ripped up the stained carpets that had dog urine all over them and put them on the front lawn with some of the other furnishings ready for the auction. Would you believe someone actually bought them? By Saturday evening, everything was sold and gone, and now, we started cleaning and getting ready for a fresh coat of paint.

Erin our daughter was not too happy about moving at first and leaving her friends in Burlington and even asked if she could move in with her friend. She came to look at the house a few weeks later and decided to move with us.

Everything has its priority, and we had to decide what came first. The horses came first. We had to put up fencing and build stalls. We converted the 2 car garage to our stable by building two box stalls in it and then had a local farmer come with a post hole digger to put up fence posts. Our friends from St Lazare, Ken and Jenny Alexander, came to help over the weekend, and we managed to fence in one paddock and build the two stalls.

Monday morning, I hooked up the horse trailer and headed back to Burlington to pick up the Boys and they were happy to see me. We were back to their new home the next morning and now the drawing that Ingrid had made became real.

We spent the next few months fixing up and painting, ready for our final move in August. All that physical work with no stress was a big plus in helping us to recharge our batteries.

 Our friends J.F. and Lise helped us once again with our move. I had helped him get a management position with Heritage after our disaster with the Haids. I had refused the position as I no longer wanted any part of home office politics, and I really did not know what I wanted to do for my next career challenge.

Ingrid and I wanted to name the property and for months we came up with all kinds of names and couldn't decide on one. One night, we were lying in bed looking through the dictionary and just having fun trying to find a suitable name and after an hour or so were getting nowhere when with my sense of humor I said "win some, lose some" and Ingrid said in old English Wynsum meant happy place. That became our estate name "Wynsum Acres", and the next day we went and had a $500 dollar sign made for the front of the property.

And what a "HAPPY PLACE IT IS".

There are times in life when you have to step back and take a break and recharge you batteries both physical and mentally.

Chapter 44

Behind every successful man is a supporting woman.

It was now the fall of 1992, and Harold Agla who was the V.P. of sales for Heritage together with J.F. made me an offer to open my own agency working from home. After some negotiation, they offered a signing bonus of $25,000 and $5,000 dollars for some marketing as an incentive to sign an agreement. There was only one clause that needed clarification and that was termination for cause; I asked what would be some of the causes and he replied fraud, bankruptcy. That clarified, we decided it was a good idea, but it meant building a sales organization from scratch, not an easy task. But, I had done so several times before, so we agreed.

As we were close to Quebec, Heritage agreed that we could have an agency there as well as Eastern Ontario.

We opened an office in Montreal and started hiring and training. It meant a commute of 1:30 hours each way.

We spent all of 1993 recruiting and training and driving and in the end did not make enough profit after all expenses that made any sense.

In January of 1994, Ingrid had an operation and while she was recuperating, my accountant and friend Tom Steynor and I did some serious brainstorming. He advised me to close the office and work from home and instead of only managing sale agents to go back to personal sales as my primary income generator. He knew that I in the past had been a super salesman. Office closed and back to what I was best at. I had forgotten that lead by example was the best way to build an agency. Within 3 months, my personal sales commissions exceeded $10,000 per month. Now was the time to recruit sales agents but not at the expense of my personal sales quotas. Training new agents took on a different role. There was some classroom but mostly riding along with me.

The agency started to grow and produce sales weekly and was soon earning overrides of almost equal to my personal sales commissions per month.

Ingrid looked after the office doing client service and the bookkeeping and I concentrated on personal sales, recruiting and training.

Every night when I would come home, she would ask how many sales I had made that day, and I would answer that I had a lousy day.

 Then, I would take the sales out of my folder and give them to her…my biggest week was 272 units being paid at $ 55.00 per unit equaled earnings that week of almost $15,000. We were back living the good life without home office politics. I was enjoying doing what I did best: selling, recruiting and training.

 For the next 6 years not much changed; we were doing well financially and living in harmony with nature on our beautiful estate. We joined two local horse clubs and went trail riding every weekend. In September, a bunch of the guys would take a week off and go camping with the horses. The first year we really roughed it, the second year we built a portable toilet, kitchen camp, took with a generator, T.V., freezer, karaoke machine and enjoyed all the comforts of home but in the wilderness.. We rode for several hours each day and both the horses and us enjoy ourselves. We even ended up written about in the local newspapers as the Cornwall cowboys.

Our menagerie of animals grew as time went on from 1 cat to 5 cats who wandered down our driveway and from one dog to 3 dogs and 4 horses. Ingrid set a rule that none of the cats could sleep on our bed and somehow they adapted.

Each year, we would win a free trip to the islands or a cruise all expenses paid for achieving sales goals. When I think of how many free trips I had enjoyed over the years, it totaled up to over 30.

In the fall of 1998 on a company cruise and while I was enjoying a relaxing massage in the hot tub, another enrollment director hopped in beside me and started to talk business. He praised my accomplishments and suggested that we merge our agencies. His name was Gary Spergel, and he had merged recently with Rob Plamondon. He praised my training abilities and tried to convince me to join them. I said I was happy the way things were and that I was not interested.

The next morning Rob Plamondon jumped into the hot tub and made the same pitch and said that our combined sales volumes would earn higher commissions. I told him to make a proposal, and I would at least look at it.

The week we got back from our trip, he sent me his proposal in the form of an agreement with all kinds of stupid clauses. I again told them that I was not interested. They persisted and suggested I write an agreement with the clauses that I wanted.

Before we merged, their combined sales volume earned them no bonuses. In the second month with my group's sales, we earned an extra $5.00 per unit. Not bad for doing nothing more than we were doing before.

I convinced two other agencies to join our merge and over the next year achieved not only full bonuses but had reached quotas to become sub distributors. As sub distributors, we would share in some of the other profits of the company, raising our income even more.

The company's policy with merges was that they would communicate to the group thru one director, and we decided that Gary would be that person. Rob Plamondon who lived in Ottawa was to do the administration for the group and would receive $2.50 per unit from us to cover costs. Commissions were paid to their company RESP sales Inc and then paid to us weekly.

When Rob saw my weekly and monthly earnings, his eyes bulged. He only had one or two agents, and he was not selling personally. He, prior to switching from CST to Heritage, had had a large group of agents, but when he made the switch, none of his agents followed him. I wondered why and discovered the reasons as time went by. From success he went to broke with a line of credit debt of around $120,000 while sitting and playing on his computer.

I asked him why he was not out selling, and he said he did not like to use the phone to make appointments. This was the downfall of many sales agents. To be successful as a sales agent you have to learn to do what others are not prepared to do.

I told him to hire a telemarketer to make appointments, and his answer was he could not afford one. I offered to loan him some money, but he was too embarrassed to accept.

I had prepared a pamphlet to be mailed to Insurance agents and suggested that that we share in the cost and hire and train these agents together and share in the overrides. We hired around 20 new agents and trained together, and this gave me the opportunity to see him in action. I did not like what I saw in his style of dealing with people. An example happened when we were in Montreal and a new agent was all excited having made her first sale of 10 units. He picked up the application, looked it over and stated it was no good. We all looked at him in shock and asked why. He said it was a monthly plan and should have been "A.I.R." annual with insurance and had referrals. What stupidity, I almost kicked his ass.

His style of management left a lot to be desired. In addition, success of our group sales went to his and Gary's head and they thought they were the ones that had made it happen.

I completed my sales manual and forms and offered to retrain all sales agents in the merged group. We held a training session in North Bay, and with my system now being used by all agents, sales increased each month.

In 2000, I was asked to do a presentation at a training seminar for all enrollment directors in Toronto. The theme was called the "Best of the Best."My presentation was on the importance of a unified training program for all agents. I presented my training manual and covered the type of training we were using for all our agents and the success we were having. The CEO from our parent company Allianz was present and liked what he heard. A few days later, I received a call from the then CEO of Heritage. Ian Glen wanted me to courier him a copy immediately as he was heading to Minneapolis to meet the head honcho who wanted to purchase my program and manual.

They ended up purchasing my manual for close to $50,000. I suggested how they should introduce it to all the other managers. Pay me a per diem and all expenses, and I would retrain every agency, or send me their regional managers and I would train them and then they could train the others. None of my suggestions were taken, and all they did was mail the manual to the agencies. The manual ended up on the shelf.

 What stupidly! They also purchased my recruiting manual for another $20,000 dollars, and Ingrid and I took a trip to Alaska and purchased a new horse trailer. Both manuals were never used. More stupidity! My training system would have reduced many of the issues of improper or inadequate training of agents which caused many problems with the various Securities Commissions.

 Now that Rob and Gary were making money and sales volumes had increased each month, I started to see and experience another side of them, something I had seen before.

Lesson learned:

Greed set in and with greed comes stupidity, and that leads me to another chapter.

Chapter 45

life is a onetime offer enjoy it!

It was now January 2004, and Ingrid had been battling cancer for over 2 years and receiving chemo every 3 weeks. She opted for treatment because our daughter Erin was expecting her second child, and she wanted to be there for the birth. The stress of her illness and stress from those two idiots was getting to me, big time.
 When I had agreed to merge my agency, I made it clear that each of us would be directly responsible for our own agents without interference. But stupidity set in, and they started to act like they owned us and our agents. It got to a point that I had my lawyer on behalf of my agency and those of Yeta and Francine send them a letter telling them to immediately stop any contact with our agents.
An example of their stupidity was when we went to arbitration, and they were to act in a fiduciary capacity on our behalf in negotiating our earned sub distributor contract. The company reneged and they on our behalf finally settled on a revenue sharing agreement where we would be paid 25 basis points on all our members' savings and interest. These idiots took ownership of the agreement and came up with terms on how we would be paid.
This was the final straw that broke any trust we had in them.
Once again, greed and stupidity showed its ugly face or should I say their true colors.
I guess power went to their heads, and I decided to no longer recruit and train new agents with Rob. Still, they acted stupidly, and in May 2004, I decided not to renew my agreement with them. Yeta and Francine did the same.
Scott McIndless one of the owners of Heritage intervened and encouraged us to resign with new clauses of no interference and clarification on our revenue sharing. We resigned even though we were not happy with these two idiots.
Ingrid took a turn for the worst the first week in February and was rushed to the hospital. The doctor wanted to send her for palliative care, but she refused and wanted to go home. We took her home. Erin and I with the help of home care and nurses looked after her for 24 hours each day, and 2 weeks later she passed away.

That was the worst 2 weeks of my life, watching her slowly fade away. I lost my best friend and love on Feb.21st. at 7.55 a.m. after waiting most of my adult life to find her, my soulmate. I was lucky to have known her for almost 30 years and married for 16.

The very first night after Ingrid passed away, Midnight our black cat jumped up on the bed 1 minute after I closed the lights and crawled up to my face and gently pawed my cheek and then curled up in the crock of my neck and slept there. He did this every night until he became ill, and I had to put him down. He sensed my loss, and this was his way of trying to comfort me.

I thought I was strong and could in time deal with the loss, but it proved too difficult, and I had to seek help with a group in Cornwall called Bereavement Counseling.

I thought if I got away from home it would help, and I booked a trip to Cuba for 2 weeks. That was the worst decision as when I arrived I was the only single amongst all the other happy couples.

Over the next 3 years, I became involved with a group that was distributing medicines to developing countries and had the opportunity to travel to nine more countries in addition to my annual company incentive trips. I travelled to Ecuador, Argentina, Chile, Viet Nam Malaysia,Thailand,Azerbaijan ,Turkey and Italy, seeing the world for free. We gave medicines to children to kill the worms caused by poor sanitation in some of those countries and other medicines where needed.

 Back in Canada, a friend of mine was going through a divorce and had registered with a few dating sites and tried to encourage me to do the same. He became an expert having met around 100 women in about 16 months and had advised me of some rules that I should use. 1. Ask for a current photo. 2. Only meet for coffee and only meet for 20 minutes. If there was no chemistry, move on. Out of the 100 he had coffee with, he finally met one and that did not even last.

As I was never one to follow rules, as I normally made them, I did the opposite of what he suggested and met some for breakfast, lunch or dinner as well as coffee. In 1 year, I chalked up some 40 meetings with not one spark of chemistry, so I decided this was not for me and decided to delete my several sites.

Most of the photos on all the sites were at least 20 years old and if you ever decide to try your hand at internet dating, I suggest you ask them to take a current photo holding up today's newspaper.

As I was deleting the last site a pop up came up for a site from China, and out of curiosity, I took a look. There were some gorgeous looking women, it had a section where you could save your favorites and I saved some. One of the prettiest was a young lady of 42 from Beijing. As I had no intention of travelling to China, I closed the site, but 2 weeks later, I decided just for the fun of it I would put up a profile.

Would you believe a few days later I received several pokes and letters and one was from the beautiful 42 years old. I wrote her back and asked her why she was interested in an older man. I had put my age as 62 figuring no one would reply if I listed my real age of 72 although I did put up a current photo. I figured a little lie wouldn't hurt as I was probably never going to travel to China. Everyone lies on all the sites so why not me.

I kept receiving several letters each week but only kept communication with 3, one being this 42 year old. I kept asking her why she was interested in an older man, and she finally answered that on looking at my photo she thought that I was a gentleman and said if I ever come to China, she would like to show me some of China's famous sites and cook dumplings for me. We communicated for months and talked about our lives. She told me about her 18 year old daughter and I about my family.

It was now December 2006, and something strange was about to happen. A new chapter in my life was being set in the stars.

I was never afraid of old age because as we age we become smarter, having had a whole bunch of life experiences. Most after mid life crises. I had always been open to new experiences and using the computer to meet other people was the new norm.

When I told friends that I was communicating with women from China they thought I was crazy. Their comments were that women from many other countries were just looking to immigrate and use marriage to a foreigner as a means.

I saw it as an experience to meet new people and have a great trip to experience and learn about their cultures and historic sites.

Lesson learned:

Don't be afraid of new experiences.

Chapter 46

Start each day with gratitude.

Strange things were about to happen. My son-in-law brought my 2 grand children to visit his parents who live 5 minutes from me. They arrived on Wednesday, and I went to see them every day for an hour or two. On Sunday, I got busy around the property and figured he would bring them over for a swim in my indoor pool or for breakfast. Sunday came and went and no visit. I knew they were to head back home Monday morning and would at least come and say goodbye. Nada! I was somewhat pissed and could not wait for Erin to get home so I could vent my anger. By late afternoon, my brain went in reality mode, and I wondered why I was so upset when all they were doing was living their own lives. I remembered back when I was busy with my life and career my parents were lucky if they saw me a few time each year.

It was getting close to Christmas, and I decided screw this, and that night I booked a flight to China. Thanks to my son in-law's action that day, I was to meet the second love of my life.

Most people never experience true love once in their lifetime, but I was about to become the luckiest man alive.

I had been communicating with 3 women, one in Shenzhen who was a 50 year old Doctor who I decided to meet first and two in Beijing: a 52 year old and Wenlian who was only 42.

I spent a week in Shenzhen seeing the sights and learning something about Chinese culture. In my mind, I had pictured China to be much like Viet Nam with old rusty bicycles, scooters and cars. Boy was I in for a surprise. New high rises were popping up everywhere, and all the cars were late models, top of the line. The city was clean, and the people reserved but friendly.

The doctor and her nephews were learning to become dance instructors and practiced morning, noon and night. I bought 2 pairs of dance shoes for $15 each and spent the week getting a few lessons. The doctor was beautiful but not my type, so on I went next to Beijing, a city at the time of 20 million residents; that's more than half of Canada's population.

I was to meet Mei Fang the 52 year old at the airport when I arrived. She was to greet me with a translator and I was to spend 5 days getting to know her.

I had arranged to meet with Wenlian the 42 year old for the last 3 days of my trip as she had offered to show me some of the famous sites.

When I exited the arrivals area, there were 3 women holding up a sign with my name. One ran behind me and took my luggage; the other 2 were from the dating agency being the translators. I did not see anyone that looked like Mei Fang's photo. I asked where she was and was told she was ill. The translator said that they had a van and would take me to my hotel. The van pulled up, and I then asked who the other woman with my luggage was. She replied that it was Wenlian the women I was to spend the last 3 days of my visit with. I turned and saw a beautiful woman all smiles and at that instant for the first time in a long time felt my heart go out to her. Instant chemistry.

We went and checked into the hotel, and then the translator, Wenlian and I went to a famous Chinese restaurant specializing serving Peking duck. Then, back to the hotel to spend time trying to communicate with each other. Wenlian spoke only a few words in English, and I spoke no Chinese. So you ask how we communicated. With our eyes, our hearts touch smiles and laughter, a first experience for both of us.

We purchased a translation machine and electronics dictionary the next day and were able to communicate that way.

Wenlian felt that it was the Gods and faith that had her come to the airport that day, and I agreed. Life had a funny way of communicating.

We spent the first few days introducing me to the cultures and famous sites in Beijing and on the 4th. Day went to see the Great Wall of China.

We took a guided tour bus with a few other tourists, two men from Mexico and a woman from Africa. Wenlian being tired from being my tour guide the past few days fell asleep on our bus ride. I turned and spoke to the men from Mexico and asked what brought them to China. They said they were custom brokers and were here on business and had decided to go see the Great wall. The asked what brought me to China and I with my sense of humor said that I came to adopt a Chinese baby. They all answered great and I then said that when I arrived the Government said that I was too old, so they gave me Wenlian instead. The woman from Africa laughed so hard she fell out of her seat.

 We spent the next several hours touring the Great wall and taking many photos before returning to Beijing.

That night we went for dinner and I of course could not read the menu, but lucky for me most dishes had photos.

I pointed at several dishes and another waitress who spoke some English was watching and came over to our table and said, I see you do not speak Chinese and your friend does not speak English; how do you communicate, and I answered we speak Japanese. She walked away confused, and we laughed.

Time for a little humor…When we were in another restaurant I asked the waiter what the population of China was and he said in broken English, 1.3 millions peoples. I than asked do you have any Chinese Jews in China. He said he did not know but would go ask the cook. He came back and said no Chinese Jews. I said impossible as Jews were everywhere, so back to the kitchen he went and again said no Chinese Jews, but we have orange Jews, apple Jews and tomato Jews. I guess I was the only Jew in China.

After dinner, I decided that my feelings for her were getting serious and that I should come clean and tell her my real age. I took a pen and paper and wrote down 72 my age and 42 her age and she took the pen from me and wrote 30. She did not understand, so I took the translation machine and explained it to her. Nothing was said that night about the difference. A few days later, she asked why I lied my age and I said that she had lied as well as her photos on the site were probably 10 years old and beautiful.

The next night we were invited for dinner at Wenlian's best friend's home. Her husband was a Major in the Chinese liberation army as was she but had recently retired. They spoke no English but had a friend who was a translator for the army join us. Her best friend's name was Shufang and his Liu. The translator's English name was Forrest that he adopted after watching the movie Forrest Gump 10 times. We communicated through the translator, and I even told a few jokes that even translated got a few laughs. Then it became more serious.

 The translator said that Wenlian liked me and wanted to get to know be better and if things worked out become part of my family. I expressed my feelings for her but said we have a few major problems. One she doesn't speak English and the other that we had a large age difference. He said that they were aware and it made no difference to Wenlian or to them.

I then said that if she were looking for a rich man it was not me. I watched as he translated and he said she was not interested in money. He explained that she was a traditional Chinese woman and only 3 things were important in her life her husband, her family and her home, in that order. I then said let me rephrase, I am not a rich man but live   a style and comfort most people would wish for and that if Wenlian and I did get together she would have everything she ever wanted: a loving husband, a family and a beautiful home.
Again, I experienced acceptance and warmth through their body language.
The table was covered with about 14 different dishes, and they had purchased a knife and fork for me. I declined and surprised them by eating with chopsticks.
I guess that I was approved as when we left Liu called me comrade Norton.
 A few days later, it was time to head back to Hong Kong and then back home. I had to spend the night at the airport hotel and could not stop thinking about Wenlian and my experience of meeting such a beautiful gentle lady. I could not sleep and wrote down my feelings, something that I had never done before. The next morning, I boarded my flight and wondered why I was heading back to an empty home.
A few months went by and we wrote to each other daily, and I decided to go back to China and see if my feeling for her were in fact real. I did not tell my son or my step daughter who I considered my daughter Erin about my feelings until I was certain myself.
So China, trip number two, planing to stay 1 month.

Chapter 47

In three words I can sum up everything I've learned in life; It goes on.   Robert Frost

Back in Beijing and to see if my feelings were in fact real and not some fantasy of a young at heart an old man. Wenlian and her 18 year old daughter Ma Li whom I was to meet for the first time met me at the airport. Here was this shy young lady who for the first time in her life was to meet potentially her future step dad and her first foreigner to boot.

She had learned some English in school but was too nervous to speak. We went to Wenlian's apartment that she had purchased a few years back, and after I freshened up, we walked down the street to a restaurant for dinner. Wenlian took my hand and I took Ma Li's and said lucky me with two beautiful ladies.

Over dinner, Ma Li lost a little of her shyness and over the next two days we were able to communicate. When she left to go back to school on Sunday night which was 12 hours away by train, she gave me a hug and said when you are coming back; I'm going to miss you. I fell in love with that little girl and hoped she would become my new daughter and decide to immigrate with her mother to Canada.

At age 72 and about to start a new family, was I nuts or what?

When I came back to Canada, I called my son and told him that I had met a woman in China and was considering possibly making her my wife. The phone went silent and then he said…you must be kidding. I said I wasn't and after some idle talk ended the conversation. A week later when I was in Toronto, we had dinner in yep! a Chinese restaurant and I said to him if his comment was because he was worried about his inheritance that he should not worry because I intended to spend it all before I left this world. He said that he was just surprised.

He was the Director of Admission for Appleby College and was traveling to Beijing at the end of the month, and I suggested he meet Wenlian and give me his opinion. They met and he too felt about her as I did.

In the meantime, back at the ranch and back to business and here strange things were about to happen; it was august 2007.

Plamondon and Spergel were still busy playing politics and still trying to stick their stupid faces in my business. I later found out that they had signed an agreement with Esther and Steve who were part of my agency even though my agreement with them had not yet expired.

I also believe that they were acting in collusion with Bruce Elliott and Jim Crocker the acting CEO in July trying to have me terminated.

The 3rd. week in August, I received a call from Bruce Elliott inviting me to home office in Toronto under the pretense to meet the new sales manager. So down the 401 I went Monday morning to arrive for a 10a.m. meeting after a 4.5 hour drive. After keeping me waiting until 10:30, Bruce and the new sales manager and I met in the conference room, and Bruce handed me a letter of termination giving me 30 days notice. I was in shock after 15 years of work building my agency and being loyal to the company that I would be treated this way.

I read the letter and then took leave of this stupid idiot and headed back home. Bruce was always referred to by all the Enrollment managers as Bruce Idiot. And he proved himself to be just that. The four partners had been at war with each other and they had decided to step back and that's when they hired Jim Crocker to run the business while their relationship cooled.

The reason given for my termination was because of a recent audit by the Quebec Securities Commission and 7 letters of complaints over the past 5 years which had been addressed. My agents, office and files were never audited. It was all bullshit invented by Bruce Idiot.

When I got in my car, I called Scott McIndless one of the partners to tell him what had happened, and he appeared shocked and said this should never have happened and that he would look into it. My termination date was extended to Oct 15th so before leaving for China I met with another partner Rob Coleman who said he would try and resolve my termination as he, being a good Christian. Believed in treating his fellow man fairly.

Prior to my final termination date, I transferred my agents to two other managers and had notified both Heritage and Plamondon and RESP by registered mail of the fact. Both ignored my letter, and Bruce Idiot sent my agents a letter stating that if they did not transfer to Plamondon the company would cancel the sponsorship of their licenses with the OSC. This in my opinion is illegal and immoral. Agents who stated that they did not want to report to Plamondon were not allowed to join another agency.

Scott McIndless was still trying to resolve this unjust termination and kept saying he was going to make it right but he had to deal with his partners who refused to approve any settlement or reverse my wrongful dismissal fearing it would set a precedent.

In the corporate world there are many different players who think only about themselves and not what is right, honest and ethical. Scott McIndless over the years proved to be a man of honor and the most ethical person I have met in my journey through the corporate jungle.

I headed back to China as we had set our wedding day for October 28th; before leaving, I gave my friend J.F. Power of Attorney to act on my behalf with Heritage. There are all kinds of challenges we experience in our lives some more difficult than others but with determination can be overcome.

Chapter 48

We can change our lives, we can do. have and be exactly what we wish.   Tony Robbins

When I was back in Beijing, my son had dinner together with us, and he met Ma Li his new sister to be. The next day he went and bought them gifts. He called me the next morning and Wenlian answered and when she handed me the phone he was laughing. I asked what was so funny; he said when she answered the phone he said "hello Mother". Funny they were both the same age. I guess that was his way of blessing our relationship.
I had asked Wenlian to become engaged at her friend's home on my previous trip and she accepted with happiness. I had had a beautiful ring and jade earrings made in the hope that she would say yes. We tried to get a visa for her to visit Canada while we were preparing immigration documents and were refused not once but 4 times.
In China, you have to apply for a marriage certificate and before it is issued both must have a complete medical. We had to travel 12 hours by train to where she was born to have this done. I have never had such a complete medical done before and when we went for the results my Dr. reviewed my results and kept saying, in broken English, good, good, good. I passed with flying colors. Wenlian's results were another story; she was diagnosed with cancer of the uterus. I was shattered and broke down in tears.
I include a letter to the Minister of Immigration from Wenlian to tell the story.
 We had planned to get married October 28, but because of her operation we postponed it until January 2008
Applying for immigration was a joke as we were put through all kinds of hoops. I hired an immigration lawyer in Montreal and even with all documents properly completed it was one hurdle after another. Not wanting to be apart from each other for lengthy periods, I made over 10 trips while waiting for immigration to do their thing. On each of my trips, we traveled to different cities and visited some of Wenlian's family and friends. Some of the cities we visited were;
Shenzhen,Harbin, Benbu, Fuyang, Shanghai, Tianjin, and Xi'an.

My son had met Jason Kenney the Minister of Immigration personally in Hong Kong at a conference and wrote him a letter supporting our marriage which he never had the decency of replying.

I then decided to meet with my local M.P. Guy Lauzon for help and he after having several meetings with Jason Kenny finally started the ball started rolling in the right direction. It took over 2 years to finally obtain their visas and landed immigration papers.

We arrived back in Canada on April 10th 2010. Why did we have to be put us through such an ordeal when drug dealers and potential terrorists seem to have no trouble getting into Canada?

I remember the morning after we arrived and were on our way to do some shopping that both Wenlian and Ma Li while driving through the village of Avonmore, commented "no peoples". A big change from Beijing. Living in the country there were more cows than people.

We visited Guy Lauzon's office to introduce him to my new family and thank him for his help and the next day a reporter came to our home and wrote an article with photos that appeared front page in the Cornwall newspaper. We were finally a family.

It was a big challenge for both Wenlian and Ma Li to adjust to life in Canada, learning English being the most difficult. They registered in and ESl program offered by the government of Ontario. The program in my opinion needs serious revisions. They teach new immigrants grammar as though they were University students. What they should be teaching is how to communicate in everyday life such as how to do banking, shopping etc. After 5 years of study most students still can't communicate but know everything about grammar.

Chapter 49

Life would be tragic if it weren't funny.   Stephen Hawking

It was now January 2008, and Wenlian was feeling much better. Her best friend Shufang arranged a church for us to be married. It was something interesting, a Jew being married in a Church with a Chinese Catholic priest officiating in Chinese. My son was best man, and Shufang was bridesmaid. Wenlian's friends and family attended. I did not understand a word that was said except my name when it was mentioned. The happiness expressed by all for us was overwhelming. When I looked over at Ma Li she was crying and happy that she now had a Dad. We had a reception at one of the famous Chinese restaurants with over 14 different dishes. Now it became waiting time for immigration to do their thing.
I was scheduled to return home on February 15th and try to settle with Heritage. On February 8^{th,} I received an email from J.F. with the result of his meeting that day with Scott McIndless and Rob Coleman who agreed to pay me my revenue sharing owed and to reassign my agents as per my registered letters to J.F. and Philippe. All of this was to be done by the time I arrived back home.
When I arrived home, nothing was settled, and it dragged on for over a month. So it was time to take matters in my own hands. I hired a wrongful dismissal lawyer, and we filed suits against Heritage and RESP. Let the games begin. Heritage and RESP filed their defense and then sued each other as to who was responsible and who would ultimately have to pay me. What stupidity. It is now 8 going on 9 years that they have dragged this on. Their lawyers are laughing all the way to the bank.
 Heritage was fighting a somewhat similar case out in Edmonton and did not want to set a president. They could have probably settled it for $400,000 back then, but stupidity had them drag the case on for 15 years, costing them I figure over $2 million dollars in legal fees. They lost at the lower court but decided to spend more money and somehow won at Appeals court. The case went all the way to the Supreme Court and guess what; they lost and have to pay yet additional costs.
 The decision by the Supreme Court will help my case big time as the court decision was that they did not act honestly and in good faith. They would have to be beyond stupid to let my case go all the way to court which would have been in

January of 2017 for 25 days.. Nine years of legal fees for them to pay. They settled 2 weeks before trial.

Stupidity and acting dishonestly has a cost and not only in money but your reputation as well.

When I look back at my extraordinary life I enjoyed everything I did, my successes and failures were all lessons learned from the School of Hard Knocks, most of which are never taught in any college or university.

Retirement for me even at age 80 is sometimes boring as I need to be creative and do things. I guess that writing my life story which is far from over yet, is the challenge I needed. I hope that some of the things I learned on my life's journey will help others to have a more fulfilling and creative life.

Lessons learned:

You can retire from your career but never retire your brain.

Affidavit:

Respectable Canadian Immigration and IAD officers:

First let me say hello to you whole heartedly! I married Norton Solomon from your country on January 11, 2008. Before my marriage, I applied several times for a visitor's visas but was refused every time, which made our life painful indeed. Nevertheless I appreciate your loyalty and seriousness to your duties!

The reasons given by your immigration officers was that they were not convinced that I would return to China after my visit and some errors which were due to some information which were caused by the understanding in communication between Mr. Norton and me.

After our marriage I applied for immigration and was refused due to some errors on my application and that the interviewer did not feel;

1. That my relationship to my husband was genuine and that we did not share a common language. I admit that at the beginning of our relationship we had much difficulty in communication but we resolved this by purchasing a translation computer and also had friends help us. Communication is not just words, it is the messages one gives to another through the heart, the eyes and touch.

 I registered in a language school and have been studying English every day since we first met. Studying a foreign language is difficult but I am confident that when I move to Canada I will improve much more quickly.

2. My husband and I had agreed not to discuss our past histories as our life together was to be a new beginning for both of us. We discussed things that we felt were important such as our families, our friends, our common interests, our love of nature and animals and our similar background in our sales careers.

3. My husband's age is not a factor in our relationship and it matters nothing to me, as he is healthy, youthful and full of energy and is the man I truly love and cherish. I am a mature 44 year old sensible woman able to distinguish my feelings of true love.

4. The discrepancies in my application for a temporary resident visa were mainly due to the difficulty in communication when completing the documents.

5. As I stated earlier my husband and I agreed not to discuss to great detail our relationships or our previous marriages, but I was aware that he loved his wife deeply and that he suffered emotionally from her death due to cancer in 2004. I am

also aware that my husband has 2 companies and had many different careers in his working life.

Our marriage is mainly owed to the help of Lady Zhang Shufang, one of my bosom friends who I have respected for years. She is a military officer who quitted the army in 1995 and now serves as a sales manager in a medium-sized pharmaceutical enterprise. She has a motherly heart and is always caring for me and paying sympathy to me. In May 2006, she introduced the transnational matchmaking company, Beijing Ouyi Cultural Exchange Co. Ltd to me (telephone: 010-68029639) through whose help I could contact with Mr. Norton in November.

When I first saw Mr. Norton's photo and knew his age in his brief introduction, I was well deposed towards him, and then I wrote a letter to him. For years I had been living with my daughter, but when she entered a college in China's Anhui Province hundreds of kilometers away from Beijing, I felt lonelier than ever and longed for love more than ever. After I wrote to Mr. Norton, I was not sure if he would reply to me. To my surprise, after several days I received a letter from him which said he was as lonely as me and longed for love like me, after which the emotional exchange between us increased quickly. I told him that if he ever decided to come to China a country incorporating the jewelries of thousands of years of history with the modern prosperities, that I would like to be a guide for him in Beijing, in China. Once again to my great surprise the gentleman arrived at this ancient oriental city across the Atlantic Ocean in January 2007, I could not find any appropriate word to describe my excited heart.

A week's getting along with each other made a good proof of the mutual favorable impression at the beginning, during which I guided him to many historical sites of Beijing, such as the Great Wall, the Palace Museum, the Ding Tombs and the Chang Tombs. Though being together with him for only a couple of days, his intension, his self-cultivation, his humor together with his vigor absorbed me so much, attachment feelings emerged between us, his age really meant nothing to me. When he returned to Canada I can't help writing lots of letters and he also replied to me with many letters to express our deep emotions. We missed each other so much that he came to Beijing four times in 2007, respectively in March, May, July and October; and three times in 2008, respectively on January 3 (left on

February 16), on April 22 (left on June 3), on September 26 (left on November 22); in 2009, he arrived in Beijing on February 3 and left on March 2. From our first meeting to the warm wedding ceremony, an excellent gentleman Mr. Zhang Hongbin interpreted for us (his cell phone: 13671315905). He was introduced to us by my friends Lady Zhang and her husband (a doctor working in China's Aerospace Ministry). I remembered in July 2007, Norton came to China and we had a dinning party in Lady Zhang's warm residence, Norton made a proposal to me with a diamond ring, which moved me so much that I can't keep back my happy tears. I accepted his proposal and we made marriage registration in the same year.

From the time we first met to the time we fell in love with each other, later to our wedding ceremony, everything embodies a perfect harmony of true love, which again kindled the flames of our lives. Language seemed so pale in communicating between us,a gesture, a glimpse could completely implicate our feelings. We respected each other, cared for each other, didn't mention the past marriage of each other only for fear that would be harmful to each other. For me, the mentioning of my past unfortunate marriage was a great pain indeed.

In 1990, my former husband began indulged in gambling which made him lose his job together with his temper. He became unreasonable, cruel and barbarous, he treated me with abuses and violence.

In October 2007, we went to the International Marriage Registration Office in Hefei, China's Anhui province to accept health inspection for marriage. Mr. Norton was very healthy but I was diagnosed with neck of uterus cancer, the "sudden storm" shocked me but I tried to calm down and made a decision to break off the engagement only for fear that my illness would be a heavy burden to him. But Mr. Norton embraced me and said definitely to me: "you are my wife! I must save you from the hands of the God of Death"! His sincere love to me deeply moved all the personnel around. I can never forget the scene when the pretty lady interpreted Mr. Norton's words for us with tears in her eyes! A leader from the registration office asked to report our love story through Medias but we declined, for we really thought we were only among thousands of ordinary true lovers.

After returning to Beijing, I was quickly sent to hospital to accept operation with the help of the couple of Ms Zhang and Doctor Liu (I couldn't keep back my tears with this memory). Before the operation I said to Lady Zhang: if the operation failed I will donate my body to the hospital to repay the society, and let my daughter be Mr. Norton's daughter as she had learned to love him as I did, to repay the emotion of my patron, my bosom friend, my husband. Thank God! The operation was a great success! Mr. Norton prolonged his stay in China and nursed me so carefully; he even hired a servicewoman to take care of me. Thanks to their care I recovered very soon. On January 11, 2008 we held our wedding ceremony in a church, in which some of his friends and his son made a special trip to take part and blessed us with my intimate friends and relatives. I thought I was the happiest woman in the world at that moment. Thank God! The more I love Mr. Norton, the more I love Canada and the Canadian people. I am an ordinary woman, a traditional wife, I want to be with Mr. Norton until the end of my life, to love him, to comfort him, to take care of him whenever he is healthy or unhealthy. We are confident to fight together with each other to get a better and healthy life.

He is my husband, my love, my family member; we miss each other despite the long distance between us. I only regret we encountered so late in life, if we met at our younger age we could have more time to take care of each other and to enjoy the happiness and beauty of life.

Every time after being refused, Mr. Norton, as a gentleman, controlled his feeling of disappointment and sadness at the Embassy but burst into tears after returning home; Every time when the departing day is near, we couldn't not help embracing each other and couldn't keep back our tears for we would feel anxious about each other in the future lonely days.

Today I write this letter hoping you upright officers could do us a favor by approving our application for me to immigrate to Canada the home of my husband.

Sincerely yours,

Wenlian Ma

Education

To be not only successful at your chosen career but continually grow and become an expert you need to continue learning new skills.
I recognized this early in my chosen career of professional selling. I attended many motivation and sales training programs over the years.
You also need to read a book a month on your chosen field and if you do this you will be so far ahead of any others in your profession and become of leader, rather than a follower.

Just for laughs;

I don't know what life would have been without my sense of humor. I have always believed it was much better to laugh than to cry and that laughter truly keeps you young and healthy.
As a young boy I was always playing pranks on friends and family and always telling jokes.
I carried my sense of humor into my business life and I believe it helped me survive many situations in the corporate jungle.
Humor helps you look at things and situations differently and reduces a lot of the daily pressures mostly created by the lack of common sense or sheer stupidly by some of your working colleagues.
I always found a way to relieve the pressure through humor.

What I learned on the journey to success:

- The School of Hard Knocks is sometimes your best teacher.
- Success in life is a series of small steps.
- When you are ready to learn new skills, the teacher will come
- It is sometime difficult to control your thoughts, but we can control how we act.
- If you become unhappy in your chosen career, move on.
- Never let you ego control who you are.
- Learn to trust yourself
- To be able to love someone else you must first learn to love yourself.
- Become best friends before you decide to tie the knot.
- Self motivation is the key to success.
- Never prejudge or assume anything.
- Never settle for average, become the best you can be.
- Never follow the crowd let them follow you.
- Be the master of your own destiny.

What sills do you need to improve to become more successful in your chosen career?

By Rank

- Listening skills
- Communication skills
- Leadership skills
- Positive thinking
- Knowledge
- Continue learning
- Think outside the box
- Common sense
- Determination
- Gratitude
- A sense of humor
- Never prejudge
- Love yourself
- Lose your ego

List of motivational speakers and sales training seminars I attended:

John Assaraf	Brian Tracy
Les Brown	Joe Vitale
Ken Blanchard	Zig Ziglar
Jack Canfield	J. Clement Stone
Stephen Covey	Dr. Wayne Dyer
Peoples Network.	Tom Hopkins
Mark Victor Hansen	Earl Nightingale
Robert Kiyosaki	Jack Lacey
Vince Lombardy	Dr. Maxwell Maltz
Og Mandino	Bob Proctor
Tony Robbins	Jim Rohn

And many others through the
- Peoples Network and motivation seminars.

List of countries and islands visited:

Counties	Visited	Counties	Visited
Alaska		Mexico	5
Argentina		Portugal	
Austria		Porto Rico	
Azerbaijan		Singapore	
Bahamas	3	South Africa	
Barbados		Thailand	
Brazil		Turkey	
Chile		Viet Nam	
China	11	Costa Rica	
Cuba		Dominion Republic	
Equador		Hawaii	
Hungary		Malaysia	
Italy		Jamaica	5

Total: 48 trips

Countries where I worked:
- Canada
- U.S.A.
- United Kingdom

From My success to your success:

1. Never let you ego control you
2. Learn from each failure
3. Become a leader
4. Always keep learning
5. Learn to listen before you speak
6. The School of Hard Knocks is your best teacher
7. Become self sufficient
8. Set goals
9. Think outside the box
10. Learn to love yourself
11. Never prejudge
12. Never assume
13. Be determined to succeed
14. Think in positive terms
15. Your attitude will determine you altitude
16. Be honest and ethical
17. Self confidence comes from knowledge
18. Learn the art of good communication
19. Practice gratitude
20. Life is for living
21. Develop a good sense of humor

My various jobs and careers:

Title	Age	Occupation
1. Grocery clerk	11	
2. Park bakery	12	
3. Our own grocery store	14	
4. Soda Jerk	15	
5. Steinberg's grocery store	17	
6. Sale of Baby Butler tables	17	Sales Rep.
7. Photographic Distributor	18	Stock clerk
8. My own restaurant	19	Owner
9. Keypunch training	21	Sales Rep
10. Miad Stone Renovations	28	Owner
11. Senior citizens home	32	Manager
12. Famous Artist Schools	32	Regional Mgr.
13. ICS Schools	36	Training Director.
14. CAFC	42	Agency Director
15. Skyseeker Aircraft	44	Owner
16. Univeristy Scholarships	47	Sales Manager
17. Childerns Education Trust	52	International V.P.
18. Personal Agency / Heritage	54	Owner